ART OF THE NEW NATURALISTS

PETER MARREN & ROBERT GILLMOR

ART OF THE
NEW NATURALISTS

FORMS FROM NATURE

Collins

This edition published in 2009 by Collins, an imprint of HarperCollins

HarperCollins, 77–85 Fulham Palace Road, London w6 8jb

www.harpercollins.co.uk

Collins is a registered trademark of HarperCollins Publishers Ltd.

First published in 2009
Reprinted with corrections

Artwork by Clifford & Rosemary Ellis, and Robert Gillmor

13 12 11 10 09
10 9 8 7 6 5 4 3 2

A catalogue record for this book is available from the British Library

ISBN 978 0 00 728471 9

Collins uses papers that are natural, renewable and recyclable products
made from wood grown in sustainable forests. The manufacturing
processes conform to the environmental regulations of the country
of origin.

Associate Publisher: Myles Archibald   Senior Editor: Julia Koppitz

Proofreader: Janet McCann   Indexer: Ben Murphy

Cover design: Heike Schüssler   Internals design: Rob Payne

Colour reproduction by Butler Tanner & Dennis
Printed and bound in Great Britain by Butler Tanner & Dennis

Contents

The modeller must develop an acute sympathy for the forms of nature. He is himself part of nature. He is a living organism and its rhythms are his rhythms. Though as an artist he will work 'parallel to, and not after, nature', he must still refresh himself, and constantly, by a sensitive observation of its forms.

Clifford and Rosemary Ellis, *Modelling for Amateurs*

Authors' Foreword and Acknowledgements

T HE NEW NATURALIST JACKETS are icons of natural history book publishing. They have graced our bookshelves for the past sixty years with a steadily expanding number of titles, all with colourful spines and imaginative designs. Arranged together, preferably on one's best bookcase and out of the light, they have been called tactile and luscious, and their impact has been compared with that of a Ming vase. They form part of the extraordinary appeal of this famous series of natural history books, long enjoyed by both naturalists and book lovers. They are, arguably, the main reason (though not the only reason) why the books are so keenly collected today. Until 1985 nearly every jacket (with a few, plain-jacketed exceptions) had been designed by the same husband-and-wife artists, Clifford and Rosemary Ellis, art teachers who also undertook freelance work. After that date every jacket to date has been designed by Robert Gillmor, one of the authors of this book. The basic design of the jackets has remained unchanged since the first titles were published in 1945.

In 1995, the other author, Peter Marren, wrote a book for the New Naturalist series that was about that series, called – what else? – *The New Naturalists*. It contained a chapter on the jackets and illustrated many of them, though (since colour was then limited to a bank of plates in the middle) necessarily mostly in monochrome. The revised edition of the book, published in 2005, contained an additional chapter, including new material on the Gillmor jackets published since 1995. Hence, when Collins invited us to write a new book dedicated entirely to the New Naturalist jackets, we did wonder whether there was much left to say.

We hope you will agree with us that there is. *The New Naturalists* described the production of the jackets in the context of the history of the series, with individual jackets brought in as examples. Here we show them one by one along with details of their production, the artistic inspiration that lay behind them, and what contemporaries (and we ourselves) thought of them. We have also reproduced as much as possible of the original artwork, sketches and other surviving background material, and with much better resolution and colour accuracy than was possible in the earlier book. We have divided the labour along the natural fault line of the book, between the Ellis jackets and the Gillmor jackets (the date of the fault line is 1985). Robert has written directly about his own designs, and Peter has tackled the Ellis jackets with the help and co-operation of members of the Ellis family. Each jacket has its own story and we have tried hard to avoid repetition by approaching each one in a different way. Much of this material has never been published before.

To vary the content still more, we invited 'guest contributors' to comment on a favourite jacket from any perspective they chose. Hence our book has been enlivened by Nick Baker's view of *The Sea Shore*, Stefan Buczacki's of *British Mammals*, Stephen Moss's of *The Redstart* and George Peterken's of *Trees, Woods and Man*. Regrettably it was not possible to include all of the guest contributions for reasons of space.

In addition, we have written a long introduction on the production of the jackets and the relationship between the artists and other key members of the New Naturalist team, notably the publisher (until 1976), William Collins, his editors and the members of the New Naturalist Board. Our account of the lives and work of Clifford and Rosemary Ellis is more detailed than that in *The New Naturalists*, and, while it is self-contained, we have tried as far as possible to avoid overlap. In particular there is more here on their related work on posters, on their love of wildlife and the countryside, and on their approach to art as teachers and practitioners.

Since 1995, new material relating to the series has come to light, notably the discovery of the early Board minutes in the papers of James Fisher, now in the archives of the Natural History Museum. These shed new light on the initial resistance to art jackets by the Board and the forceful role of Billy Collins not only in insisting on their commission but in the close interest he took in their production, the carefully nurtured patron-and-client relations between publisher and artists. The discovery of some of the original artwork from which the jackets were prepared, and more details of the triangular relationship of artist, blockmaker and printer, sheds light on the constant battle between artistic standards, economic constraints and practical realities. The more one studies the correspondence, the more miraculous it seems that the outcome in most cases was at least satisfactory.

Interest in this series has grown over the past fifteen years. When *The New Naturalists* was being written, in 1994, new titles had slowed to a trickle. The series appeared to be running out of steam; ten years before that the publishers had seriously considered winding it down. Today, by contrast, there are up to four new titles a year (about the maximum the system can cope with) and they are now in full colour. Sales are healthier (though nothing like the extraordinary print-runs of the 1940s), and the scientific quality is as high as ever, with outstanding new contributions by luminaries such as Oliver Rackham, Stefan Buczacki, Adam Watson, Sam Berry and George Peterken. There is a thriving New Naturalist Collectors Club and a Collins-run website with a lively and often outspoken forum. The Folio Society commissioned a boxed set of the first ten titles, and the publishers now offer to print-on-demand for those missing titles on the shelf. There are times when it all feels like a dream. We hope that all those who are enjoying this late blossoming of the evergreen series will also find much to enjoy in this book. We hope it will also make new friends among those interested in commercial art and design or who simply love beautiful books.

We have people to thank. The book would have been impossible in this form without the interest and co-operation of Penelope and Charlotte Ellis, Clifford and Rosemary's daughters. They have been most generous in allowing us to copy material in private archives and in sharing their knowledge of their mother and father's work. They made extensive and thorough comments on the full text, and it is incomparably the better for their contribution. Sadly, Charlotte Ellis died while this book was in production.

We owe a great debt to Martin Charles, who scanned or photographed images of much of the archival material for us. We were lucky to be able to count on his expertise, and infinite care and patience, in producing such excellent images for publication.

We are also indebted to Professor Michael Twyman for his extensive knowledge of lithographic printing and Professor Martin Meade for information about the artistic milieu of Clifford and Rosemary. We thank Tim Bernhard for sharing his incomparable knowledge of the series and also in arranging for the missing minutes to be photocopied and generously lending them to us before he had had a chance to read them. We are also grateful for his comments on the jackets from an artistic perspective. Tim has also contributed a guest appreciation of two of his favourite jackets, *Mountain & Moorlands* and *Sea-Birds*.

We thank David Kings for copying artwork for *Waders* for us, and our other guest writers, Nick Baker (*The Sea Shore*), Andrew Branson (*The Hawfinch*), Stefan Buczacki (*British Mammals*), Mike Dilger (*The New Forest*), Richard Lewington (*Butterflies*), Stephen Moss (*The Redstart*), Desmond Nethersole-Thompson (*The Greenshank*), Mark Parsons (*Moths*), David Streeter (*Fungi*) and George Peterken (*Trees, Woods and Man*).

Finally we thank Myles Archibald for commissioning the book, tracking down elusive artwork in the Collins Glasgow warehouse and seeing it through to publication with the assistance of the New Naturalist series editor, Julia Koppitz.

Introduction

THE COLLINS NEW NATURALIST LIBRARY is a publishing phenomenon. It started during World War II (like National Parks and nature conservation planning) and rolled on unstoppably, decade after decade, far beyond the plans or expectations.

If you have picked this book up, our guess is that you have at least heard of the series and probably know something about it. Perhaps you came across it at school or university, and have some favourite titles on your shelves. Possibly you are a full-fledged New Naturalist collector. Maybe you even own a full set, now taking up an entire bookcase from floor to ceiling, along with the 22 New Naturalist monographs and the ill-fated single-volume New Naturalist magazine (we know of one or two hardcore collectors who are seeking to own every edition). Or perhaps you are just intrigued about why there should be a whole book about so humble a thing as a book jacket. Either way, do read on.

It would be bad manners, as well as unwarranted, to assume that you know all about the series already and so launch straight into the story of the jackets. The full story of the New Naturalist library, of those that wrote them, and the team that set it all in motion, and kept those titles rolling, can be found in Peter Marren's *The New Naturalists* (always apt to be out of print but fairly easily found secondhand, especially in the revised edition). Here we can at least offer a summary of what the books are about, and why they are held in high regard. If this is familiar ground already, skip this bit.

At the time of writing there are 110 titles in the mainstream New Naturalist library. There are also 22 titles in the long out-of-print monograph series devoted to a particular species or more specialised subject. Today's marketing economies decree that books are never in print for long unless they turn out to be bestsellers; the life in print for a New Naturalist nowadays is only a few years, and often less (it depends on how long the hardback run takes to sell out). But many older New Naturalist titles were kept in print from the date of publication to the 1970s or '80s, and some bookshops displayed them all together.

These books are unusual. They are halfway between being popular and academic, and are at once interested in the minutiae of life and the big picture. Taken together they offer a survey of the wildlife and scenery of a single country over half a century that is probably unique. The library was the brainchild of William Collins (1900–1976), managing director of the family publishing business, who conceived an ambition to publish a series on natural history that would establish his company as the leading natural history publisher. The series would take full advantage of the latest developments in colour photography and in the natural sciences. On the publishing side he had established a successful partnership with a printing company, Adprint, with whom he launched the wartime hit series, *Britain in Pictures*. The partnership was to continue into the early years of the New Naturalists, in which Adprint (until they dropped out in 1950) was to commission illustrations, maps and diagrams.

Collins decided he needed a team of distinguished naturalists to draw up a list of titles, find the right authors for them, and to ensure the highest scientific and literary standards. This became the New Naturalist Board (also called the New Naturalist Committee). Collins persuaded Julian Huxley, one of Britain's leading zoologists, to head the team, along with James Fisher, a young ornithologist whose book, *Watching Birds*, had been a wartime bestseller. The pair was joined by the bird photographer Eric Hosking, the botanist John Gilmour, and the geographer, Dudley Stamp, with either Collins himself or, increasingly, a deputy, officiating. The Board had its first meeting in early 1943, and thereafter met more or less monthly in a succession of temporary premises in war-torn London. Each of the editors was responsible for the titles within their professional knowledge, and they took a small royalty from the books for their services. They were loyal to the series and its aims, and, one suspects, shared a sense of mission born of the war and the hopes of the new Britain that would follow it. The original Board oversaw the developing series for 23 years without change until the death of Dudley Stamp in 1966. The last of them, Eric Hosking, served the series for nearly half a century.

The credo of the series was spelt out opposite to the title page of every book. Its aim was 'to interest the general reader in the wildlife of Britain by recapturing the enquiring spirit of the old naturalists'. This reads a little oddly now – who exactly were these 'old naturalists'? The style sounds like James Fisher's and he was probably thinking primarily of people like Gilbert White, the parson of Selborne, whose approach to nature was based on asking himself intelligent questions and trying to find out the answer by observation and simple experiment: 'the enquiring spirit'. In the view of some, 'nature study' had since degenerated into trophy hunting and collecting: pinning, stuffing, pressing and mounting. Fisher wanted to reignite the old spark. The New Naturalists, that is, the modern successors of Gilbert White, would be best served by a correspondingly new kind of book, dedicated to 'maintaining a high standard of accuracy combined with clarity of exposition in presenting the results of modern scientific research'. Above all, they would be about live animals, not dead ones.

It all sounds rather formidable and challenging. Natural history was to be revitalised by the latest developments in genetics, behaviour and, above all, ecology and conservation, simplified as far as possible for a lay public, but never over-simplified. In practice it meant that many titles were written, with varying degrees of literary skill, by university professors and other academics; some even became set books for the Open University and other educational institutions in the 1960s and '70s, and were published in paperback to match student budgets. Did the books succeed in their lofty aims? Some did. A few were too dry or overspecialised, and quite often the academic authors strained too hard to be impersonal even when describing their own, sometimes mould-breaking, research. At their best, though, with *The Sea Shore*, say, or *The Wild Orchids of Britain*, there is a happy and constructive meeting of new science and old natural history. And some of the best books in the series were written by 'amateur naturalists', like W. S. Bristowe's *The World of Spiders*, or, among the monographs, Ernest Neal's *The Badger*.

The New Naturalist 'credo' promised that wild animals, birds and plants would be 'portrayed in the full beauty of their natural colours, by the latest methods of colour photography and reproduction' (this promise was quietly dropped once the colour content dropped to almost zero!). The phrasing sounds old-fashioned now, but in 1945 colour film was scarce, and so slow that it could only capture wildlife if it remained obligingly motionless. For the colour plates of *Butterflies*, published in 1945, live butterflies were said to have been photographed for the first time in colour against a realistic (but not necessarily natural) background.

The first New Naturalist titles were *Butterflies* by E. B. Ford and *London's Natural History* by R. S. R. Fitter. This was to be a numbered series, and, since things never go exactly to plan, these were numbers 1 and 3. There was never any particular order to the titles. The reason why New Naturalist number 1 happened to be *Butterflies* was that it was the first book to be completed. *London's Natural History* was not even on the original wish list. Its author, Richard Fitter, had been asked to write about the Thames Valley but said he preferred to do a book on London. There was, in fact, a fair amount of randomness to the whole process. Many planned books about the forthcoming National Parks or about bird habitats, or even major topics like fish or ferns, were never completed (or not until decades later). Sometimes the Board responded positively to a suggestion, for example for a title about bumblebees or the folklore of birds, especially in the early days when it seemed that the public was ready for almost any subject so long as it was attractively presented.

In the immediate postwar years the New Naturalists sold like hot cakes. Most of the first titles had initial print-runs of 20,000 or even 30,000, and so are still common (though in variable condition) in secondhand shops or on the internet. From about 1950, the sales slackened, partly because of the rising costs of printing, especially colour printing, and also, probably, because the series had lost its initial lustre and punch. The average print-run of titles published in the 1950s was only half that of the '40s, while the total sales of most of the new titles published after 1960 were in only four figures (and remain so today).

What, then, made this the longest-running and most highly regarded natural history series of them all? A good start was important, permeated by that messianic wartime vision of the future. The books had things to offer that were new and exciting: colour photography, new ways of seeing wildlife, most notably in the context of their homes and habitats, glimpses of the vast worlds of ecology and evolution behind the lives of familiar animals and plants. The books themselves were attractive and produced with care with hard-wearing buckram bindings, gold-blocking of the title and colophon, and the good printing and layout for which Collins was famous. Being numbered and in standard livery, they were collectible, and became more and more so as the titles accumulated. They were reasonably priced, at 16 shillings in 1945. They sat nicely in the hand and handled well, neither springing shut nor falling flat. They even (or is this just us?) smelled nice, of hayfields in late summer. And then there were the jackets …

The jackets. We come to it at last. The first New Naturalist jackets were bold, imaginative and quirky, quite outside the usual run of natural history book design. They lacked detail or line and yet there was something about them that struck the eye and invited the curious to take down the book and open it. If there was anything remotely like them in the bookshop, it certainly wasn't on the natural history shelves. On each of the early titles, the letters 'C&RE' appear, followed by the date. Who or what, some must have wondered, was C&RE? Let's begin with that.

C&RE: A SHORT BIOGRAPHY

The letters C&RE on the New Naturalist book jackets stand for Clifford and Rosemary Ellis; their names are usually spelt out in full on the rear fly leaf. Today these jackets are their best-known work, though book lovers may know some of their other jackets before and after the war, for the Collins Countryside series in the 1970s, or their design for John Betjeman's *Collins Guide to English Parish Churches*. Within the art world they are remembered more as innovative teachers, Clifford Ellis having run the Academy of Art at Corsham Court for a quarter of a century with his wife Rosemary as a leading member of the staff. But information about them is quite hard to come by. There is no biography, and very little about them on the internet. I attempted a short biography of 'C&RE' (as I shall call them) and their work for my book, *The New Naturalists* (1995), with the help and co-operation of Rosemary and her two daughters, Penelope and Charlotte. This more detailed account builds on that foundation, and, once again, I have relied heavily on information and comments from the family.

Clifford and Rosemary Ellis were at once husband and wife and an artistic partnership. Their collaboration began in 1931, the year of their marriage, and

ABOVE *Carting: two straining horses, carter and part of a hay wagon* by Clifford Ellis, 1925. On rough paper in pencil and sepia wash (27.7 × 41.6 cm).

subsequently almost all their published freelance work is signed jointly. By the time the New Naturalist jackets were designed they had taken to using the cipher C&RE to express their joint authorship. Such consistent use of a joint cipher is unusual, and needs a little explanation. The initials were put in alphabetical order, not out of any sense of seniority. In the 1930s and '40s, 'R' sometimes preceded 'C' to indicate where she was the initiator and had carried out most of the work. Penelope Ellis explained that its point was that they considered their freelance design work to be the product of two minds 'collaborating in flexible harmony'. They seemingly never discussed with a third party who did what, and their work on book jackets was usually done behind closed doors. Both were distinctive artists and respected each other's styles and preferences. The handwriting on the surviving New Naturalist artwork jackets is invariably Clifford's (as is most but not all of the correspondence), but it would be wrong to assume that the hand that held the brush was normally his. The final artwork was only the last stage in a lengthy process of sketching and thinking, selecting and eliminating, and the creative impulse behind the design was, as they saw it, an equal joint effort. 'C&RE' indicates a rare and complete fusion of creative thought.

Clifford Wilson Ellis was born in Bognor, Sussex on 1 March 1907, the eldest of four children born to John and Annie Ellis. Artistic talent ran in the Ellis family.

His father was a commercial artist, while his paternal grandfather, William Blackman Ellis, was not only a painter and naturalist but, for a time, a skilled commercial taxidermist. 'Grandfather Ellis' was also a countryman in the old-fashioned sense with a deep understanding of the land and its wildlife (in Clifford's boyhood he kept a tame otter which was allowed to roam over part of his house in Arundel).

Another well-known artist in the family was Clifford's 'Uncle Ralph', Ralph Gordon Ellis (1885–1963), a landscape painter and designer of inn signs. During his long career he designed hundreds of signs, especially for the Chichester-based Henty & Constable brewery. One of them, for 'The Mayflower' in Portsmouth, was the subject of a postage stamp in 2003. A blue plaque now marks his former home on Maltravers Street, Arundel. Around 1950, Clifford took his younger daughter, Charlotte, to Uncle Ralph's studio, and she remembers him explaining to them both how inn signs are designed to make an impact from a distance, well above eye level, and how that was a very different matter from being seen close to, on the easel. Clifford, in turn, was to become fascinated by the way subjects are transformed when seen at different angles or against different backgrounds.

In 1916, his father having joined the Royal Engineers and been sent to France on active service, the nine-year-old Clifford spent several formative months with his grandparents at Arundel while his mother, expecting another baby, coped with her two small children at her parents' home in Highbury. On vividly recalled walks with Grandfather Ellis, Clifford discovered nature and wildlife in the unspoiled West Sussex countryside, including the magnificent great park of Arundel Castle with its herds of deer – an experience, enhanced on subsequent holidays, that made a profound and lasting impression on him. From Grandfather Ellis he learned how to preserve and stuff animals, as well as to arrange their pose and painted backdrop to make them look as lifelike as possible. There are family memories of the young Clifford boiling small mammals to reveal their skeletons, and, once, his causing consternation by fainting halfway through the dissection of a rabbit. Clifford also acquired an assortment of slightly unorthodox pets: lizards, frogs and stick insects.

In November 1916, following the birth of his sister, Clifford rejoined his mother and family in Highbury to sit the Junior County Scholarship which enabled him to attend the Dame Alice Owens Boys' School in Finsbury. He was by now what his later colleague and fellow teacher Colin Thompson described as 'a voracious reader', a habit he kept up all his life. He became a frequent visitor to London Zoo which he used as a kind of living reference library to study the way the animals moved and behaved. Throughout his life he enjoyed visiting zoos, exhibitions, galleries and museums, both at home and abroad, filing away perceptions and images in his mind. 'Clifford was deeply interested in visual communication,' recalled Charlotte. 'His visual memory was extensive and nearly always deadly accurate.' The jacket of *British Seals*, for example, was based on his memories of the postures of seals at London Zoo.

RIGHT Clifford and Rosemary Ellis (1937), in their studio with the cartoon for the mosaic floor for the British Pavilion, Paris Exhibition of 1937. Photo: Kate Collinson/Norman Parkinson Studio (Kate Collinson was Rosemary Ellis's sister).

After leaving school, Clifford attended two full-time courses in London art schools, first St Martin's College of Art, then the Regent Street Polytechnic, before taking University of London postgraduate diploma courses in art history and art education – where he was particularly inspired by the innovative ideas of Marion Richardson. All this time his perceptions of art were expanding. From his family he had thoroughly absorbed the William Morris-derived notion of 'art for all' – the infusion of artistic principles in the arts and crafts, as expressed in commercial art such as posters and advertisements. As far as he was concerned, natural history, art, educational theory and graphic design were interlinked aspects of a whole. Visits

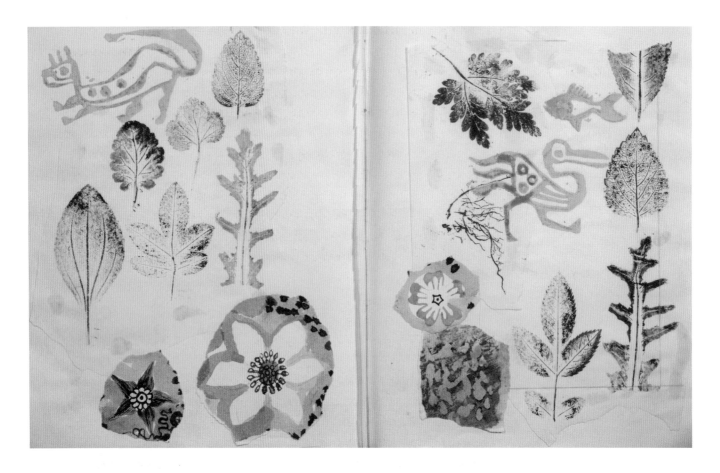

ABOVE Leaves from Rosemary Ellis's scrapbook of c. 1944–5, made up of fragments of designs, collage and printed, in watercolour, pen and printing ink, double spread (23 × 37 cm).

to exhibitions by progressive artists like Paul Cézanne, or the opportunity of seeing Paul Klee paintings brought to lectures by Roger Fry, opened his eyes to their freshness of colour and the visual impact of forms reduced to their essentials.

Having been a student teacher at the Regent Street Polytechnic, in 1928 Clifford became a full-time member of staff there. He was placed in charge of the first-year students and taught perspective – a technique and skill he mastered with ease and whose historical development always fascinated him. One of his young students there was his future wife, Rosemary Collinson. Born in Totteridge, North London in 1910, Rosemary, like Clifford, came from a family of craftsmen and artists. Her grandfather was F. W. Collinson, a leading designer of art furniture and co-founder of the fashionably aesthetic firm of Collinson & Lock. Her father, Frank Graham Collinson, trained as an artist and cabinet maker before going into the family firm and subsequently founding his own furniture business, Frank Collinson & Co, Designs for Decorations & Furniture.

Rosemary was also related to a famous writer, her maternal uncle, Edward Clerihew Bentley (1875–1956) – 'Uncle Jack' as Rosemary knew him – the leader writer and author of innovative modern detective novels, notably *Trent's Last Case*, who, while still at school, had invented the 'clerihew', the humorous rhyming form of verse named after him. His subsequent published volumes of clerihews had great popular success and many eminent emulators.

Rosemary's father had joined the Volunteers where he rose to become colonel, a rank he retained on their later absorption into the Territorial Army. He served in the Great War at that rank, initially in training but soon enough on service, first in France and then in Italy. There, having survived the war, he succumbed to the terrible worldwide flu epidemic in 1919. Rosemary, with her sisters and brothers, had been taken by their mother to live with her parents in their large house at Netley Marsh in the New Forest. Rosemary therefore had a similar, if lengthier, formative experience to Clifford's, of a wartime country childhood. She, too, developed a deep fascination for nature and animals in and around the Forest, and always retained particularly fond and vivid memories of her grandfather's pigs and rare-breed herd of Gloucester park cattle. After the war Rosemary and her younger sister moved with their widowed mother to London; their elder siblings had, by then, flown the nest.

PICTURES FROM THE THIRTIES

Clifford and Rosemary married in 1931. Rosemary brought to the artistic partnership an instinctive eye for colour, tone and composition; she had a quick mind and the ability to master a new medium at speed. They shared the same open, enquiring spirit, branching out at various times into sculpture, mosaic (including an important commission for the design and laying of the mosaic floor for the British pavilion at the Paris Exhibition in 1937), ceramics and modelling, needlework and mural painting. But their distinctive sense of colour and design is nowhere better seen than in the posters they designed in the 1930s. Posters in the 1920s and '30s were often designed with great care and dash, even those that were advertising a product. They became an art form pursued by progressive artists on both sides of the Atlantic in which an image was used to convey a powerful message. Successful poster art needed to say something clearly, simply and, above all, memorably. Distilling a sometimes complex idea into a single image exercised the brain quite as much as a large canvas or sculpture. In their day many leading artists designed posters in the prevailing spirit of 'art for all', as a means of bringing art centre-stage into the lives of ordinary people. Among the rising generation of British artists designing posters and book jackets at this time were Ben Nicholson, Graham Sutherland, Edward Bawden, Eric Ravilious, Barnett Freedman, Paul Nash and the American graphic designer, Edward McKnight Kauffer – more or less a Who's Who of contemporary British art. The 1930s were, arguably, the high noon of poster art in Britain. Every image, said the artist John Berger, 'embodies a way of seeing' (Bernstein, 1992). The artist's job was to see something as if for the first time, and to communicate that insight.

Clifford and Rosemary designed many posters during the 1930s, for the Empire Marketing Board, for Shell-Mex and BP Ltd, for the great Frank Pick, inspirational

Chief Executive of the London Passenger Transport Board, and for the Post Office, as well as lithographs for Lyon's Corner House ('the Teashop Lithographs'), all of them institutions that found reasons for persuading top artists to produce work for what one called 'the art gallery of the street'. Paul Rennie described the Ellis's poster style as 'painterly', effectively building up their designs as a succession of separate colour printings. 'These combined the expressive style of the early design reformers with a Fauvist-inspired colour palette' (Rennie, 2008).

Some of their posters were intended for specific events, such as test matches, while others were part of a public service for educational and cultural establishments such as museums, galleries and gardens. One of their first major commissions, from 1932, advertised Whipsnade Zoo above a banner suggesting that BP Petrol was the ideal medium for your car journey to the zoo. Designed to catch the eye of a passer-by (the original poster measured 45 by 30 inches), it is an unforgettable image of four wolves staring wide-eyed from the trees with not a cage or bar in sight. Like so much of their work, this image was based on close on-the-spot observation. Rosemary's memory was of the young Clifford and herself walking to Whipsnade over the downs by night, and choosing a dry ditch to take a nap, waking to find the wolves staring at them.

Winter Visitors

FIRST TEST MATCH · LORD'S

ENGLAND
v
WEST INDIES

JUNE 24 26 27

Station LORDS or by bus or coach

THIRD TEST MATCH · THE OVAL

ENGLAND v
WEST INDIES

AUGUST 19 21 22

Station OVAL or by bus or tram

come out to live!

BUY A SEASON TICKET

Another important sponsor of commercial art was Shell, which later showcased some of the best poster design from the 1920s and '30s in *The Shell Poster Book* (1992). The man responsible, a counterpart to Frank Pick at London Transport, was Jack Beddington, who persuaded the company to allow artists to produce designs in their own way with a minimum of commercial interference. Together, the Shell collection advertises not so much the corporate brand as the British landscape and way of life, while, seemingly incidentally, presenting Shell in the guise of a patron of artistic good taste. One of C&RE's Shell designs, dated 1934, shows Lower Slaughter Mill in Gloucestershire as an image of a lost rural England of millstreams, sleepy willows and a village lane empty of cars, painted in pure greens, ochres and reds. It is signed 'Rosemary and Clifford Ellis', and hence was a Rosemary-initiated design. Another poster, a joint work done the same year, has an array of antique artefacts, including a grinning stone gargoyle, within a ruined abbey and assures us with a wink that 'Antiquaries Prefer Shell'.

It is quite easy to spot a poster by Clifford and Rosemary Ellis even without the cipher. The colours are fresh, bright and without outlines, the designs simple and bold, and the foregrounds and backgrounds juxtaposed in a characteristic way. They often express an idea rather than a product. With hindsight one might discern elements of the New Naturalist jackets in their poster of a trout fisher's tackle over the legend 'Anglers prefer Shell'. Their taste for open-air scenes of nature is still more evident in a quartet of metre-tall images commissioned by London Transport, entitled simply, 'Wood', 'Heath', 'Down' and 'River', each symbolised by a lively graphic representation of a wild bird, respectively a green woodpecker, an owl, a kestrel and a heron. In the background of each one, people are having fun: ramblers ask a shepherd for directions; a man and his girl choose a spot for their picnic; a dad gives his child a piggy-back ride. Nature is accessible and enhances life.

From 1934 to 1937, the couple also designed dust jackets for novels published by Jonathan Cape, having caught the eye of a young editor, Ruth Atkinson. These were printed in a similar way to a poster, by lithography and in three colours, and they were executed in a modernist style that brings together intriguing elements from the story. Clifford and Rosemary always liked to read the book before they started work on the jacket. I have never heard of *North-West by North* by Dora Birtles, or *The White Farm* by Geraint Goodwin, let alone read them, but their striking jackets would certainly make me want to take up the book and open it.

By 1936, the couple, with their year-old first child, Penelope, had moved to Bath where they had both been offered teaching posts. Rosemary became the art teacher at the Royal School for Daughters of officers of the Army on Lansdown, while Clifford took up an appointment as assistant master at the Bath School of

Art, then part of the city's Technical College. Initially he taught art to 12- to 14-year-olds preparing for local trades skills, such as bookbinding, painting and decorating. He must have made a great impression because, two years later, he was appointed headmaster.

London Transport window bill, *Summer Is Flying*, by C&RE, 1938, printed by Johnson, Riddle & Co, London (25.5 × 73 cm).

Meanwhile, shortly after their arrival in Bath, Clifford and Rosemary joined the Bath Society of Artists, where they were soon elected onto the committee for the Society's annual exhibitions. Among the many artists they came to know was the painter, and sometime pupil of Sickert, Paul Ayshford, Lord Methuen (1886 – 1974), as well as the famous 'grand old man of British painting' himself, Walter Sickert. The now aged and venerable Sickert, with his third wife, the painter Therese Lessore, had moved to Bathampton in 1938, where they lived in what was to prove their last home at St George's Hill. Ailing but still active and ever quizzical, Sickert proposed to Clifford in March 1939 that he teach at the Art School once a week, free of charge. His offer was eagerly accepted, and Sickert would talk and reminisce for two hours every Friday to Clifford's students, continuing to do so until his health failed him in the early years of the war. Clifford and Rosemary were to be of great help to Therese Lessore in the hard task of caring for Sickert during his final illness up to his death in January 1942.

SUMMER IS FLYING

In 1939 *Modelling for Amateurs* by Clifford and Rosemary Ellis was published in the Studio 'How to do It' series (a revised edition was published, again in two formats in 1945). By then, the Ellises were at the heart of the local art world, teaching, and producing innovative freelance work. Then World War II intervened.

CLIFFORD AND ROSEMARY'S WAR

The art school remained operational throughout the war, even after being transferred to and then bombed out of its wartime Green Park buildings during the 'Baedeker' air raids on Bath. Remarkably, under the circumstances, a fine if less spacious house was made available in Sydney Place. Clifford saw the war in a positive light as an opportunity for sharing 'a deeper and richer life' through the dispensation of the arts. When war was declared, Clifford was 32 and unlikely to be called up. But he certainly did his bit. He joined the local Home Guard (and said long afterwards that *Dad's Army* got it spot on). He also worked as a camouflage officer and instructor, working out how to make factories look like ordinary rows of terraced houses when seen from the air. Moreover he was invited to contribute to the 'Recording Britain' programme instigated by Kenneth Clark. The programme gave official work at home to many artists not commissioned into the services under the auspices of CEMA (Council for the Encouragement of Music and the Arts). In this context, Clifford made a pictorial record of Bath's bomb-damaged buildings of architectural importance, as well as of the city's beautiful iron railings and gates before they were removed, supposedly for turning into tanks and planes. Clifford succeeded in saving some of the best examples, but most of the Georgian, Regency and Victorian railings removed in Bath, having (like those removed from London and other cities) proved useless for military purposes, were later dumped in the North Sea. In addition to running the Art School and his continued active involvement in the Bath Society of Artists, Clifford also founded the Bath Art Club in 1940 where, throughout the war on Monday evenings, he sustained a remarkably wide-ranging and inspired programme of notable guest lecturers, including Kenneth Clark, John Summerson, Nikolaus Pevsner, John Piper, Geoffrey Grigson and Lawrence Binyon.

Rosemary, meanwhile, was pursuing her teaching at the Royal School. However, since its buildings, like so many in Bath, had been requisitioned by the Admiralty for the duration of the war, the School had been evacuated to Longleat House, near Frome. This meant that Rosemary underwent a lengthy daily round trip by bus and

bike (she hid her bicycle behind a telephone kiosk near the bus stop). She nonetheless found time to make some delightful pen-and-wash studies of the girls' incongruous occupation of the magnificent Longleat interiors, and of buildings in and around Bath. And, by the end of the war, she and Clifford had their second daughter, Charlotte, born in 1945.

The art school premises at Sydney Place were cramped, and Clifford worried that, as people returned from the war, they

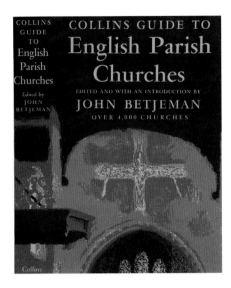 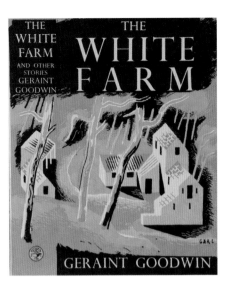 

ABOVE Book jacket designed by
C&RE and printed in four
colours by Collins, published in
1958. John Betjeman liked it.

ABOVE RIGHT Jackets designed
for Jonathan Cape and Collins by
C&RE, printed in three colours.

LEFT London Transport window
bill advertising London Zoo by
C&RE, 1939, printed by
Dangerfield Printing Co Ltd,
London (25.5 × 31.5 cm).

might very well be taken over for housing. It occurred to him that were the Bath
School of Art to become a residential art college it did not need to be in the middle
of the city, and that a suitable rural location would in many ways be preferable. And,
as it happened, Lord Methuen's country seat at Corsham Court, a fine Elizabethan
mansion, altered and enlarged in the eighteenth century, was about to be returned
to its owner after being used by the War Department as a convalescent home for
injured troops.

'It was one of those flukes which doesn't occur very often,' recalled Clifford. 'It
was a matter of finding somewhere … with a bit more space than we had got then at
Sydney Place … I made a mental note of likely places and Corsham Court was top of
the list. I telephoned Lord Methuen and asked him what he was going to do when
he got rid of the convalescent hospital and he said he wished he knew, so we
arranged to meet the next day, and in those few hours of optimism when the war
ended, the whole thing was fixed up in something like a week. It couldn't have been
done earlier and it couldn't have been done later. So we offered ourselves as a place
for students to come the following September, and they came, and we started.'
(from a taped interview with CE, 1981).

To run what became the Bath Academy of Art, Clifford had turned down a
proffered Chair of Fine Art at Durham University. In the words of the Prospectus
of 1953–4, he 'hoped that the existing school might contribute "depth" and the new
school "breadth", to an Academy which as a whole might be greater than its parts'.
The four-year course, leading to the Ministry's National Diploma in Design, was
based on an unusually liberal and broad-based scheme of teaching, which would
include not only the visual arts but music, dancing and drama, as well as various
branches of science and technology. In response to the vast national demand for
teachers (secondary education having been guaranteed for all under the 1944 Butler
Education Act), he was also able to provide a training course for art teachers; by
the time the course closed in 1967, some 600 art teachers had passed through
the college.

The Academy opened as a residential college in September 1946 with Clifford as its Principal and Rosemary as an active member of staff (her role changed from 'art education' in the 1950s to 'senior year tutor', 'senior lecturer' and 'chairman of the board of studies' in the 1960s, specialising in audio-visual studies and visual communication). The Ellises moved into a flat in part of the top floor of the east wing.

'Pike' lithograph (with added watercolour) of a pike and arrowhead lilies signed by Clifford Ellis, shown at West Riding Spring in 1973 (77 × 56.5 cm).

Clifford ran the Bath Academy of Art at Corsham for a quarter of a century, from 1946 until his retirement in 1972, aged 65. He did so with enthusiasm and vigour, and with a syllabus strongly flavoured with Clifford's inner conviction that 'arts are the staple of the fulfilled life'. One teacher had been warned before arriving that Clifford 'had a lot of funny ideas. Corsham was trying to teach too many things all at once … the students were only dabbling in drawing and painting and sculpture' (Thompson). To this, Clifford might have replied that his idea of teaching art was to practise it. He wished to draw from his students the same sense of vocation that he felt himself, 'like a gardener tending his plants'. He was ahead of his time in believing in teaching by suggestion, by opening windows and encouraging the student to develop their own burgeoning talent.

To further this aim, Clifford resolved to restrict the number of students to a maximum of 250 or so. He also assembled an impressive number of full- and part-time teachers who were, like himself, practising artists, some of whom were, or later became, famous. The distinguished painter William Scott (1913–1989) was the part-time senior painting master, while Kenneth Armitage (1916–2002), who notably made his name with his bronze figures, was in charge of sculpture. The painter-potter James Tower (1919–1988) taught all aspects of pottery and ceramic art, and took students on archaeological digs. A taste of cosmopolitan Europe was brought by the Warsaw-born painter Peter Potworowski (1898–1962). Howard Hodgkin (b. 1932), first a student, taught part-time for eleven years before concentrating full-time on his own painting. At different times, amongst other staff were influential artists like Peter Lanyon (1918–1964), Adrian Heath (1920–1992) and Gillian Ayres (b. 1930). Among such a stellar gathering, the sense one gets from the recollections of Corsham teachers and students is of a bucolic idyll in the Wiltshire countryside among a group of like-minded masters and apprentices.

The surroundings lent themselves to nature study, which was always close to Clifford's heart. The Court was set in grounds that recalled his beloved boyhood Arundel Park. The academic syllabus included, in the early years at least, botany, biology and geology, and natural forms always remained a key component of pre-diploma and design courses. In keeping with these precepts, Clifford created various gardens at nearby Beechfield, which had also been acquired for the Academy. His 'bog garden' lent itself to the first-hand study of various botanical 'forms', and there were also aviaries where the students could observe and sketch small birds, pheasants, ducks and geese.

Although they could both put a name to most of the birds and wild flowers they saw, Clifford and Rosemary were more interested in the shapes and designs of nature, with their energy, strength and boundless variety, and the way they feed the artist's imagination. 'The artist,' said Clifford, 'must develop an acute sympathy for the forms of nature. He is himself part of nature. He is a living organism and its rhythms are his rhythms. Though, as an artist, he will work "parallel to, and not after nature", he must still refresh himself, and constantly, by a sensitive observation of its forms' (Ellis, 1945).

Clifford and Rosemary's book, *Modelling for Amateurs*, includes not only lively renditions of nature but natural objects themselves: 'Notice the full roundness of the fox's skull, and then the sudden ridge that runs down it: or the tough but delicate curve of the deer's jaw ... ,' they wrote. 'Compare the three shells on the left – see what they have in common and yet how freshly and surprisingly different is each of the individual spirals. Then turn the book sideways and upside down and look at them again. There will be surprises. Then instead of looking at the shells look at the shapes of the background.'

Clifford was remembered at Corsham as a visionary, a man with the confidence to tread his own path and flavour the syllabus with his own artistic credo. Never part of the art establishment, he was seen as a crank in some quarters and never received the national honour many thought he deserved (Brown, 1988). In thanking Clifford and Rosemary for making 'a seemingly redundant Mansion into a virile Academy of Art', Lord Methuen felt they had 'welded Bath to the structure [ie. the house] for another hundred years' and proved that 'these historic houses have a future, when used for the benefit of those who come under their influence and who are receptive to their principles of life' (private letter, 19.7.1972). Alas, long after the Ellises' departure, changing times finally caught up with the Bath Academy of Art. In 1983, it was amalgamated with the Bath College of Higher Education, and, three years later, lost the unique ambience of Corsham Court. It is now called the Bath School of Art and Design within Bath Spa University. Beechfield, where the students learned to paint and turn their pots, is now a 'gracious' housing development, with the house and former stable block converted into flats.

RETIREMENT YEARS

Clifford and Rosemary had bought a house in a Wiltshire village just below the downs where the family moved in 1972. One sunny room was allocated as a studio, and another became home to Clifford's large and wide-ranging book collection. Below the house, Clifford planted a new valley garden with an artist's eye. He continued to teach, part-time, on adult education courses, and he and Rosemary collaborated with others on the texts of educational books for children. Rosemary pursued her photographic interests and, with her elder daughter, Penelope, produced numerous sets of large prints illustrating aspects of the natural and man-made world. They also, of course, continued to design the New Naturalist book jackets as well as some of those of the Collins Countryside series. Both their daughters qualified, Penelope as a sculptor at the Slade and subsequently as a teacher at the Institute of Education at London University, and Charlotte as an

architect at the Regent Street Polytechnic.

Clifford died, after a short illness, 19 March 1985, aged 78. Rosemary and Penelope continued to live in the same house until Rosemary's death, aged 87, on Ascension Day, 21 May 1998. They are buried in the same grave on a grassy plot in the village cemetery below the downs under a headstone (carved by Penelope with some advice from Charlotte), inscribed simply 'C&RE' with their respective dates.

THE NEW NATURALIST JACKETS

The House of Collins was not, until the New Naturalist library appeared, noted for imaginative jackets for their non-fiction titles. For the great wartime series, *Britain in Pictures*, the jacket had simply repeated the pattern stamped on the boards; it did little more than provide the title of the book and a common branding. The lowly role of such 'wrappers' is summed up in a piece of doggerel the New Naturalist collector Roger Long once found inscribed on the wrapper of a book of verse:

This outer wrap is only meant
To keep my coat from detriment.
Please take it off, and let me show
The better one I wear below.

The New Naturalists were different. The war was still on when Clifford and Rosemary designed their first New Naturalist jackets, *Butterflies* and *London's Natural History*, in autumn 1944. The first dozen or so were done at home at Lansdown Road, Bath, and the later ones, until 1972, at Corsham Court or while on family holidays, often abroad. The jackets were all based on first-hand research, and, as often as not, involved journeys to look for suitable material for a jacket. For example, they made a special trip to Dartmoor, and, later on, visited both Orkney and (Clifford alone) Shetland for their respective jackets. Sometimes material was found much closer to home, such as for *Lords and Ladies* and the bee orchid for the discarded jacket of *Wild Orchids* which were found growing by the north walk at Corsham Court. For *The Pollination of Flowers*, Clifford visited the Hatherley Laboratories at Exeter University to see Michael Proctor and hear about his work on pollination photography. Each jacket was the result of research, sketches, colour experiments, and much thought before arriving at a suitably arresting image.

The basic form of the New Naturalist jacket was worked out on the very first jacket, *Butterflies*, and continues, barely changed, 65 years later. Its distinctive style has no obvious link to other book jackets published at the time by Collins, and it seems likely, though nothing we have seen explicitly says so, that every element on it – the coloured band with the title in nearly all cases spelt out in white, the oval on the spine containing the New Naturalist 'colophon', and the wrap-around, lithographic image itself – was thought out by Clifford and Rosemary Ellis. They also designed the distinctive New Naturalist symbol of two conjoined letters N, together with the charming idea of a small symbolic image where the letters meet. Similarly, they designed the special monograph colophon of 'NMN', which was worked out with pencil on the commissioning letter from Collins. The idea of a numbered series was, however, probably taken from the long-running *Britain in Pictures* series published by Collins and Adprint between 1941 and 1945. It was implicit from the start that this would be another numbered 'library' of books.

Art jackets were not new in 1944; Clifford and Rosemary had themselves designed jackets for Jonathan Cape. The first book jackets that aimed to be more than pictorial paper bags had appeared in the early 20th century, and by the 1930s a new generation of artists like Edward Bawden and Eric Ravilious had begun to specialise in the medium, producing jackets that look vivid and fresh even today. Adventurous jackets were not confined to works of fiction. For the *English Life* series published by Batsford, Brian Cook produced dazzling wrap-around designs that exploited a new process for overlaying coloured transparent inks of high intensity that were, in his words, 'blatant, bizarre, strident and unreal' (Cook, 1987). Encouraged by craftsman-printers like Thomas Griffits, lithography became a popular printing method to produce jackets of brilliant colour and bold graphic form. World War II and rationing brought most of this to a screeching halt, and the bookshops of the immediate postwar world were a good deal dingier than before. Fortunately the firm of Collins was a printer as well as a publisher, and had stocks in hand to make a splash with the new series.

While the public were used to seeing art jackets around books, they might have been surprised to see them on books about butterflies and geology. It would be an exaggeration to say that the New Naturalist jackets created a sensation, but they certainly impressed the booksellers and William Collins was much encouraged by the positive trade response to the first two Ellis jackets. The colours were bright but not garish, reminiscent of lithographic prints, and produced using matt inks on rough-surfaced paper. They strongly implied something new and in which Collins took great pride. It was unusual, even then, for jackets to be completely hand-drawn, right down to the series colophon and title lettering. They caught the eye, as intended, but the books also sat sweetly together on the shelf, more and more so as the series expanded. Perhaps few jackets had paid such close attention to the spine and the way it fitted into the rest of the design. They might have been more stunning still if the artists had been allowed to carry on the design over to the back of the book, as Brian Cook did on the Batsford books, but that space was needed to advertise, and later to list other titles in the series.

To summarise the New Naturalist jacket:

1. It portrayed the contents of the book in bold forms and bright colours, printed by craft methods. The arts-and-craft look was intensified by the exquisite hand-lettering of the early titles.

2. The design was 'bled off', that is, there was no frame or margin. It ran over the edge in every direction except one, where the design petered over on to the back, ending not in a mechanical line but in brushstrokes.

3. The jackets were, at least initially, prepared for printing by skilled lithographers used to interpreting the ideas of an artist.

4. The book was easy and pleasant to handle because the design was printed on slightly rough paper and did not slip. For the same reason it fitted snugly to the buckram binding of the book.

5. The jackets showed 'forms of nature' interpreted by sympathetic and knowledgeable artists that gave them vitality and inner life. They were intended to intrigue. They were not intended to shock, but perhaps, especially at first, they did.

WINNING ROUND THE SCIENTISTS

My book, *The New Naturalists*, describes in some detail how William Collins conceived this ground-breaking series of nature books, and the board of celebrity scientists which he set up to commission books and oversee their production. The committee was headed by Julian Huxley, perhaps then Britain's best-known biologist, but the key personality on it was his energetic protégé, James Fisher. The young Fisher was full of fire about the advance of natural history in postwar Britain; he was in great demand for natural history radio programmes in the 1940s and '50s. He, perhaps more than the others, was convinced of the potential mass appeal of illustrated books on natural history and their importance in promoting interest in birds and other wildlife. He was later to become a great influence on natural history publishing, not least as a senior advisor and book commissioner for Collins.

The idea of fancy jackets for the New Naturalist books appears to have originated in the mind of Ruth Atkinson, who joined the firm in 1943 and soon became a trusted advisor to the chairman, William ('Billy') Collins. During the 1930s she had worked as a book editor for Jonathan Cape where, among other things, she commissioned artists to design jackets. Clifford and Rosemary Ellis had been among her clients; she had been impressed by their work and, it seems, had already got to know them well. On 20 July 1944, Ruth wrote to the Ellises to tell them about the forthcoming series and ask whether they now felt 'at all inclined to do book jackets'. The new books would have 'a great many illustrations', she went on, 'and I thought that you would do lovely jackets for them.' But, she warned, 'there are a great many people whom the jacket must please: besides Mr Collins, the editorial committee of this series and the producers of it, Messrs Adprint.' She invited them to 'work out a rough, for say the first title', and hoped to be able to discuss it further with them (RA to C&RE, 20.7.44).

The Ellises' response was to invite her to Bath for the weekend where, during a 'deliciously comfortable and peaceful stay', Ruth persuaded C&RE to try out a colour sketch for the jacket of *Butterflies* by E. B. Ford. As was to become the rule, she sent them some material and 'pulls' of plates from the book to provide an idea of its

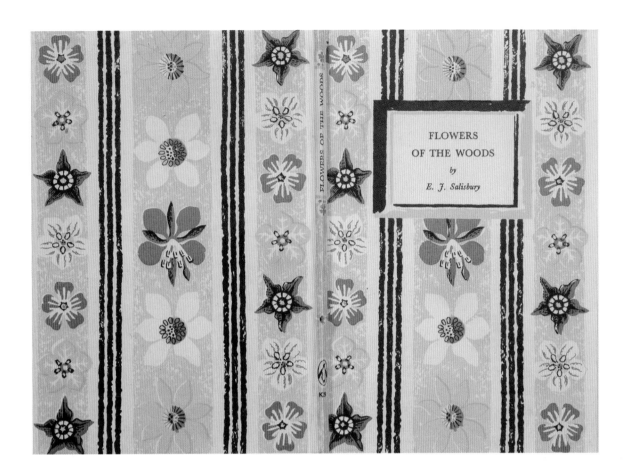

FLOWERS
OF THE WOODS
by
E. J. Salisbury

nature and contents. By September 1944, the artists had produced an arresting
design based on the Swallowtail butterfly and its caterpillar, drawn at twice the size
of the printed jacket. At the same time they had also, presumably at Ruth Atkinson's
request, produced alternative jacket designs, two of which incorporated a small
photograph. Ruth especially liked those, but Billy Collins preferred the Swallowtail.
(RA to C&RE, 18.9.44: 'he likes the two without the photographs best – I like those
with the photographs'). She added that Collins had liked the Ellises' work 'better
than anything else which has been submitted'. Another artist had also been working
on the New Naturalist jackets, 'but he has had to give it up' (RA to C&RE, 8.9.44); who
that artist was we have been unable to discover.

Billy Collins had indeed liked the design. It is a fair guess that he had looked for
an original and arresting style of jacket from the start and had given his blessing
to Ruth's apparently solo venture. Collins saw the job of the jackets to sell books,
and hence they were his responsibility and not that of the New Naturalist Board,
whose purpose was, rather, to achieve high and consistent scientific standards for
the series. He ignored (though tactfully) the Board's strongly expressed preference
for photographic jackets, and invited the Ellises to design jackets for the first six
books. They were offered 12 guineas per jacket and three guineas extra for the
specially designed colophon. Their fees later rose more or less in line with
inflation, but were always modest.

The first design for a New Naturalist colophon, created by C&RE in 1944, shown here almost full size.

The decision, therefore, to commission C&RE was made by Billy Collins alone and in the teeth of opposition. The (newly discovered) Board minutes grumpily note that 'it had been agreed that Messrs Collins, knowing the Editors' views on the subject, would be entirely responsible for the production of the Wrapper' (NN Board, 9.9.45). 'It really is a question of pleasing Mr Collins', Ruth Atkinson had told the Ellises, 'and not the naturalists' (RA to CE, 17.10.44).

The Board might have had a stronger case for a photographic jacket if they had some strong photographs to show. But in 1945, good colour photographs of wildlife in natural surroundings were still rare; nearly all the colour photographs in the first New Naturalist titles had to be commissioned specially with Adprint's precious stocks of American Kodak. *Butterflies* included some ground-breaking shots of live butterflies taken in colour by Sam Beaufoy, but even so it is hard to find even one that would make a satisfactory book jacket.

Early in 1945, James Fisher had been deputised by the Board to visit Clifford and Rosemary in Bath to find out more about their ideas and techniques. 'I hope you get on well with Fisher and win him over to the idea of non-photographic jackets which will be a major achievement', wrote Ruth to Clifford, perhaps a little nervously (RA to CE, 22.1.45). Fisher, it seems, was indeed won over, but other members of the Board, especially Julian Huxley, Eric Hosking and John Gilmour, were not, at least not at first. Hosking, in particular, felt that the credo of the series, and its unique selling point of specially taken colour photographs, demanded a photographic jacket. After viewing the first few jackets, seemingly with tight lips, the Board gradually grew to admire them, and, by 1948, they were all full of praise for that of *The Badger*.

For the time being, however, when advance copies of the first two New Naturalists lay on the table before them (with photographers invited in to record the occasion), this is all the minutes have to say about it: 'Dr Huxley said he still did not like the idea of non-photographic wrappers but as he understood that it was impossible to change now, would it be possible for future volumes to try out some other artist as well?' Eric Hosking suggested Jack Armitage as a possible alternative. John Gilmour asked that in future the editors, if not the authors, be shown the jacket designs before the books were printed, which Collins agreed to. He [i.e. Collins] added that 'he was quite willing later on to try out some other artist but that no series of wrappers which Collins had produced had ever been so successful as these with booksellers and others, and that he was of the opinion that the artists who are designing them were first class and great experts' (NN Board meeting, 15.11.45).

That was the end of the matter. The channel of communication between artist and publishers lay not with the Board but almost entirely with Collins and his editors, first Ruth Atkinson and later Raleigh Trevelyan, Jean Whitcombe, Patricia ('Patsy') Cohen, Michael Walter, Libby Hoseason and Robert MacDonald. Billy Collins, one suspects, had no intention of 'trying out' any other artist, whatever he might have said to Huxley. He had 'for more than thirty years been unfailing in his generous and kind encouragement to us', wrote Clifford and Rosemary after Collins' death in 1976. 'To us it was an ideal patron and artist relationship' (C&RE to Lady Collins, 22.9.76).

The Ellises were commissioned to design jackets for the first six books and then another six, after which their commission became open-ended. The artists admired the series and felt committed to it. Despite a few hiccups along the way, most notably when the standard of printing fell in the early 1950s, they enjoyed the work. Including the monographs, C&RE produced 86 jacket designs over 40 years, plus many more for books that, for one reason or another, never reached publication stage. After Clifford's death, Rosemary recalled how designing the jackets made 'such a refreshing change to the problems of running an academy. The manuscript and the wherewithal for doing a jacket often came on holiday with us and I have happy memories of sitting outside a tent with Clifford in some remote part of

Europe working on the designs' (RE to Crispin Fisher, 1985).

It is surely Clifford and Rosemary Ellis, as much as anyone, who established the 'brand image' of the New Naturalist series, and helped to make it the most long-running, and latterly also the most collectable, library of books in the natural history world. In return, the books have kept the work of C&RE alive and made their images some of the most eye-catching and distinctive in modern publishing.

HOW THE JACKETS WERE PRODUCED

There is no written record of the exact process in which the first New Naturalist jackets were printed, and there are unlikely to be any living witnesses to remember. We know, however, that they were printed by Baynard Press in London and by offset lithography. Further clues survive among the correspondence, which, though as it survives is one-sided and often cryptic, reveals at least that the method was based on photography. Using their great experience of the lithographic medium, C&RE always did their level best to make life as easy as possible for the printer.

Lithography is a method of printing from a flat surface. The name comes from Greek words meaning 'stone-writing', for lithographic prints traditionally used a flat stone surface to transfer the image from artwork to paper. The artist drew with a crayon on a slab of carefully prepared limestone. After the drawing has been prepared, prints are taken from it by dampening the stone and charging it with greasy printing ink. The technique is based on the principle that oil and water do not mix. From the early years of the 20th century the process was mechanised by the 'flat-bed offset machine', in which the paper received the print from an intermediary process, a smooth rubber roller. Offset printing prepared the ground for the flowering of poster art in which graphic designs from serious artists appeared in the hallways of railway stations and London Underground, and on advertisement hoardings originally intended to hide unsightly development.

The advantage of lithography is that it enables the artist's work to be reproduced in limitless numbers without any alteration of the original design. Among the outstanding printers and proponents of colour lithography were Curwen Press and Baynard Press, both of which had close links with the London art schools and printed posters by contemporary artists, including Clifford and Rosemary Ellis. From 1935, Baynard Press employed one of the best-known craftsman-printers of the day, Thomas Edgar Griffits (1883–1957), known as 'the Indefatigable Griffits', who shared the secrets of his craft in two mainstream books, *The Technique of Colour Printing by Lithography* (1948) and *The Rudiments of Lithography* (1956). Griffits was a skilled interpreter or 'translator' of other artists' work. He was also something of a lithographic missionary.

Once Collins had decided to use the Ellis designs, the question was where to print them. During October 1944, Ruth Atkinson costed the alternatives of

ABOVE Colour sketch for the jacket of the unpublished *Ponds, Pools and Puddles* by C&RE, mid-1970s. This title, also known as *Ponds, Pools and Protozoa*, was to have been Sir Alister Hardy's third contribution to the series, after the two *Open Sea* books. By complete contrast with the vast expanses of ocean, this book would be devoted to 'the microscopic life of the little waters'. Hardy approved the colour sketch, although he had reservations about the much-magnified organisms shown beneath the surface of the pond. Unfortunately, Hardy never found time to complete the book, though it remained a desired title and is now slowly heading towards publication.

OPPOSITE Colour separations for *Ponds, Pools and Puddles*.

photogravure or lithography before deciding on the latter. She met Thomas Griffits, who advised her that the most cost-effective way of printing the jackets would be 'photo-litho with a deep etch for the line', and for the prints to be made on rough paper (presumably using matt printing inks). He was also 'most decided about the fewer colours the better'. Hence Clifford and Rosemary designed most of their New Naturalist jackets as 'camera-ready artwork' in four colours or fewer, relying on tones and overlaps to tease out more colours. Finally, Griffits advised that they produce artwork at exactly the same size of the printed jacket, for otherwise 'a great deal of the subtlety of detail' would be lost (remarks conveyed to C&RE by Ruth Atkinson, undated but late 1944).

It may seem surprising that the House of Collins, which was a printer as well as a publisher, did not decide to print the jackets in-house. The probable reason is that C&RE's designs were closer to an art print than most book jacket designs, and that this required the skills of experienced art printers. Clifford no doubt convinced Ruth Atkinson that their work needed an experienced 'translator'. The Ellis designs required exact colours printed in the right order, and the characteristically fuzzy outline of their colours needed an experienced interpreter.

The printer normally worked from the three primary colours, plus black. Mixing these was a craft in itself. For example, wrote Thomas Griffits in 1956, 'by adding a little orange, green or violet to any of the primaries a less harsh and more pleasant hue is obtained.' Darkening a colour with black was to be avoided as it detracted from its luminosity. Lighter colours were obtained not by mixing in white but by stippling the plate or adding chalk. Further colours could be obtained by overprinting, but it was important to print these in the correct order. For example, green printed on top of violet could produce (unlikely as it might sound) an attractive pale grey, while printing violet on top of green might achieve nothing but a muddier shade of violet. Certain colours go well together and enhance one another, while others, like green-blue next to blue, have the reverse effect.

For each jacket C&RE made a full colour design using water-based paint: mainly gouache but sometimes with additional watercolours, and incorporating the white of the paper. With the design came instructions pencilled underneath for the exact colours, and the order in which they should be printed. They prepared separate artwork for the series colophon and the title lettering. On most of the books published in the 1940s, the title and name of the author was hand-lettered on the title band, while for nearly every title up to No. 24 (*Flowers of the Coast*) the colophon was individualised with a symbol of the book's contents. Several jackets were produced by different techniques during a brief period of experimentation in 1950–1. From 1970, the jackets were produced by a completely different method.

In some cases the original artwork of the New Naturalist jackets has survived (and is reproduced for the first time in this book). Some retain registration marks which indicate that the artwork was photographed by a special plate camera. Each colour would be separated by the blockmaker as 'film positives' and then transferred on to

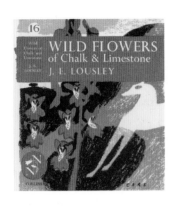

ABOVE Tricky jackets: cost-cutting experiments were made over the printing of *Wild Flowers of Chalk & Limestone* and *Birds & Men* in 1950–51.

a lithographic plate. A comparison between the surviving Ellis artwork and the printed jacket shows how faithful the results could be in the hands of experienced operators.

Jackets that were to be printed by the thousand in a single production run required power presses. By 1945, automatically fed printing machines could run at high speeds ranging from 2,500 to 5,000 impressions per hour. All but one of the first 15 New Naturalist jackets were printed by Baynard Press (the exception was *The Art of Botanical Illustration* which was probably done in-house). The colours of these jackets are wonderfully harmonious, with subtle, pleasing tones quite unlike the brighter but harsher 'Pantone' inks of the 1970s. Six proof copies of each jacket were normally made, one of which was sent to the artists for their approval, while another was circulated at New Naturalist Board meetings.

By 1950, however, Collins was looking elsewhere to print the jackets. The costs of book production, and colour printing in particular, had soared while sales were falling. Furthermore, Collins's alliance with Adprint had come to a premature end in 1950 when the latter found the series 'no longer an economic proposition'. The Collins printing factory in Glasgow was clamouring to do the job. The then editor, Raleigh Trevelyan, was minded to try it out for the next jacket, *Wild Flowers of Chalk & Limestone*. It would require changes in the way the jackets were prepared, and opened the way to a period of unsuccessful experimentation. The results were at first lamentable. The printers could not reproduce the colours accurately enough without using screens that diminished their impact. The artists thereupon drew the design afresh as colour separations on plastic transparencies, and, when that did not work either, directly on to the printing plate.

After yet more trouble finding alternative ways of printing the jacket of *Birds & Men*, Clifford dropped a strong hint that they were getting fed up with the whole business. Billy Collins wisely stepped in and instructed the editor to print the jacket in the usual way. Even so, the artists were asked to try again with colour separations for *The Greenshank* and *An Angler's Entomology*, in the first case using only two colours. From 1951, the blocks for the jackets were no longer prepared by Baynard Press but by Odhams Ltd, a Watford-based 'gravure printing house' which owned modern offset presses. The blocks were then sent to the Collins factory for printing. The method now relied on what the correspondence refers to as the 'line method'. At first it was what Clifford called 'a flukey business' (CE, 12.1.52) resulting in harsh gradations with 'everything very sharp and black' (the jacket of *The Greenshank* being the worst example). Nor could the new printers match Baynard Press's skill in mixing and matching colours. The jacket of *Flowers of the Coast* was a dismal failure, while the artwork of *The Sea Coast* and *The Weald* was tampered with and 'mutilated' by the blockmakers.

The standard of printing soon began to improve, and there are fewer problems on record from the mid-1950s onwards, though the fine touch and delicacy of colour that marked the earlier jackets is lacking. More problems surfaced in the

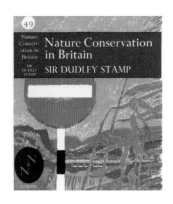

ABOVE Good and bad solutions: The jacket of *Nature Conservation in Britain* was printed with the help of a colour-deadening screen, while *Man & Birds* was the first jacket to benefit from combining sets of colour separations.

1960s, when the gap between the artists' intentions and the printer's capacity to meet them seemed to widen again. On the *Nature Conservation* jacket, for example, the printers seem to have given up and used a coarse screen for the overlaps, while for *Grass and Grasslands* they printed the colours in the wrong order.

Dissatisfaction with these jackets led to a major overhaul in the way the jackets were produced and printed. By now the artist could indicate the exact tone or shade required by reference to a 'Pantone' number. The Ellises decided that better results could be obtained by using 'colour separations' since these enabled the printers to reproduce the artwork with greater precision, and allowed the artists greater freedom to create bold and colourful designs. It involved them in the difficult task of producing a jacket which would be seen only after it was proofed (Clifford memorably compared it with reading the musical score of a quartet). Fortunately C&RE were experienced hands at such 'reading', in which four sets of brushwork in black paint on white watercolour paper would in due course become a well-realised colour jacket. By 1970, this craft-based method was a rarity in the field of commercial art. Michael Walter, the experienced Collins editor of the time, said that the Ellis hand-brushed artwork separations were the only non-mechanical colour separations (apart from maps) he had ever seen.

Brighter and more transparent printing inks meant brighter, more luminous jackets and allowed the artists to adopt a looser style in which dry brushwork produced the characteristic fuzzy-edged colour masses of what one might call the Ellis's late period. To help the printers, and also allow the Collins editor to get at least an idea of how the printed jacket should look, they also provided a colour sketch (which was in some cases a close match to the printed jacket). The new method of production by colour separations continued until the last Ellis jacket, *The Natural History of Orkney*.

When Robert Gillmor came to design the jackets in 1985, he used a similar technique, though drawing the colour separations on sheets of clear plastic instead of watercolour paper. From 1986, the jackets were printed by the offset machines of Radavion Press in Reading, sufficiently close to his workplace for Gillmor to be present at each printing and so able to make any necessary last-minute adjustments and to choose the proof that best matched his conception. After Robert Gillmor moved to Norfolk in 1998, the jackets were printed in much the same way (and with Robert looking on) by the Norwich-based Saxon Photolitho Ltd until 2004 when the jackets began to be printed overseas. Over time, Robert has varied his technique, using linocuts more and more to add vitality to the designs (Gillmor, 2006). These changes are discussed in the main text under the appropriate jacket.

The Jackets by Clifford & Rosemary Ellis

Butterflies

E. B. Ford, 1945

OPPOSITE The first submitted design for *Butterflies* with hand lettering on watercolour paper by C&RE, 1944. It was painted at twice the size of the printed jacket (37.2 × 31 cm).

The dust jacket of *Butterflies* must be one of the best-known images in the world of natural history publishing – so familiar in fact that it is hard to recapture how unusual it must have seemed when the book was first put on sale in November 1945. For those used to more conventional book jackets, this design, in which the caterpillar is so much more prominent than the adult butterfly, both conveyed in terms of form and colour rather than strict scientific fidelity, must have raised a few eyebrows. C&RE's first jacket design certainly helped to underline the 'new' in New Naturalist.

The prototype of the *Butterflies* jacket was a painting of September 1944. Twice the size of the printed jacket, the artists used gouache and watercolour paint on thick, rough-surfaced watercolour paper. At this stage the Ellises probably did not know that they would be restricted to four colours (including black).

Later the design was redrawn to the same size as the printed jacket in response to recommended printing requirements. Completed by January 1945, C&RE made a number of modifications, bringing the butterflies closer and making more of the distant trees and windmill. The blue was deepened to enable the title lettering to show more clearly. Perhaps few readers would have spotted that the orange colour enclosing the book's number is the caterpillar's defensive organ, known as an osmeterium.

William Collins had 'asked a great many people about this jacket. He likes the original rough and the smaller redrawing of it', Ruth Atkinson went on, 'but has received a good deal of criticism at your using a Swallow-Tail which is a very rare butterfly in England I am told. He would like you to do the design again, using another butterfly – possibly the Dark Green Fretillary [sic]. Mr Collins hates to ask you to begin all over again but as we are quite definitely not using the design you finally submitted, I think it might be easier to suggest a third alternative for this title' (RA to CE, 8.2.45).

Butterflies
E.B.FORD

Collins

It seems, then, that there were three versions of the jacket design for the first New Naturalist, the original rough, the modified design drawn at jacket size, and a third version with the fritillary that C&RE produced and sent to Collins by February 1945. By then, however, Billy Collins had changed his mind and decided to stick with the Swallowtail design after all. He was now 'absolutely happy' about the jacket, and commented that he had personally 'always liked the Swallow-Tail, and I hope you will do this. I do not think that the criticism of its being rather rare matters,' he added, 'and I do not think one could get anything more lovely' (WC to CE, 16.2.45). 'We are rather keen to get this design as soon as possible', he went on, 'as it is ahead of the other MSS in production'. Four days later, Ruth Atkinson was thanking Clifford for 'the finished design for *Butterflies*... I like it very much and am delighted to have it so quickly and am sending it off to Mr Griffits today' (RA to CE, 20.2.45).

The modified design was in four colours, blue, yellow, orange and black, with shades of green produced by overlaps. White was let in by leaving the appropriate areas blank. Clifford was disappointed by the proof: the blue was not deep enough for the white title lettering to stand out distinctly, the greys and greens were insufficiently distinct, and the yellow had come out too orange. Not all these faults were overcome on the printed jacket. Nonetheless, Ruth expressed herself 'extremely pleased' by it, and Billy Collins felt 'more pleased than ever with the wrapper now I see it on a book' (WC to CE, 5.6.45).

The *Butterflies* jacket was, in effect, a trial run. The initial problems with the printing were never fully overcome, and the effect is somewhat tentative and wishy-washy. In 1962, the printers decided to deepen the colours, especially the blue of the title band, by using a screening process, but the result was to cast a greyish smog over the whole design, making the jacket look rather grubby. But what mattered far more was the impact of the design: the first Ellis jacket proclaimed that these books were different: serious, modern, grown-up, challenging, new. For that message the last thing anyone wanted was another pretty butterfly on another pretty flower.

Richard Lewington, the wildlife illustrator, writes: 'For the jacket of a book about British butterflies the Swallowtail is a prime candidate as a subject. It's large, rare and most people would recognise it, even if they had never seen one patrolling the Norfolk Broads. Its bold markings make it the butterfly equivalent of the avocet or the giant panda. The graphic image on the jacket of *Butterflies* is, however, surprising in that it is the equally striking caterpillar that takes centre stage, with the two butterflies in flight confined to the middle distance. To add colour and drama, the caterpillar's orange osmeterium, used to scare predators, is inflated. I like the balance of the design, which also gives a hint of the butterfly's habitat with the windmill in the distance, but feel the spine lets it down. It is too abstract and gives no clue as to the subject matter of the book.'

British Game

2

Brian Vesey-Fitzgerald, 1945

OPPOSITE Artwork for *British Game*, 1945. The hand-lettered title and colophon were designed separately and combined by the printer.

It was probably the striking jacket of *British Game* that settled the argument about whether to use photographs or artwork for the New Naturalist dust jackets. On 7 December 1944, William Collins professed himself 'absolutely delighted with the partridge for *British Game*. I think it is quite lovely in every way' (WC to CE, 7.12.44). He was commenting on the artists' 'rough', twice the size of the printed jacket and against a grey background. On the finished design, sent in on 24 January, the artists substituted 'umber brown' for grey. Collins preferred the rough and hoped that they 'would some day … be able to use the original colour scheme on another design'.

This is a bolder, more confident jacket than *Butterflies*. An approximately life-size English partridge dominates the scene, its head twisted back above the title band, perhaps in tribute to the old masters of bird portraiture who showed large birds in this awkward attitude in order to fit them on the plate without reduction. The partridge is running towards the spine over an open down, its body language and alert eye (beautifully observed) suggesting alarm. Several birds in its covey have already taken off – wispy, almost abstract shapes on the left front and spine – and our bird will doubtless follow them shortly. The glory of the design lies in the colours: the ochre, terracotta and pale grey create a sepia-tinted landscape, a timeless vision of the old England of rolling hills, hedgerows, weed-fringed arable fields and abundant game that, in the immediate postwar period, might have caused a twinge of nostalgia.

Copies of the jacket exist where the design has been mistakenly repeated on the back against an umber background. Possibly they were rejects brought in for the last remaining stocks of *British Game* in the late 1950s or 1960s to avoid the expense of printing a new batch.

This jacket gave Collins the idea of a 'big illustration-book of individual birds on the lines of Gould' which he wanted James Fisher to write and Clifford Ellis to illustrate. He was still talking about it a month after the jacket was accepted, and a month is a long time in publishing.

London's Natural History

R. S. R. Fitter, 1945

The anonymous designer of the jacket of *London's Birds*, 1949, by the same author, borrowed C&RE's idea of juxtaposing seagulls and the dome of St Paul's Cathedral.

The first design for *London's Natural History* (originally titled *Natural History of London*), completed by October 1944, featured ducks on a pond. William Collins liked it and preferred it to the *Butterflies* jacket (at the time he had said of the latter, 'nothing could be more lovely'; evidently it could). Soon afterwards C&RE produced a new version, keeping the idea of reflections in water, but substituting a livelier bird: a gull. The duck lived on inside the oval on the spine on the NN logo.

London's Natural History needed an image that said, clearly and unambiguously: London. C&RE found it in the dome of St Paul's, an icon of the City's suffering during the Blitz, only four years previously. But instead of the actual dome they showed its reflection in water, possibly just a puddle, possibly the River Thames (bombing and house clearance would just about have made that possible in 1945). Everyone liked the design, but, wrote Ruth Atkinson on 8 February 1945, 'Both Mr Huxley and Mr Fisher … would like you to include the crescent which appears behind the bird's eye. This I understand will turn it into a black headed gull, which they think very suitable.'

The design allowed the artists to create interesting watery effects, with flying gulls reflected in the ripples as flickers of white. The jacket is beautifully printed in soft browns and greys, with the only bright colour, red, reserved for the bird's bill, legs and eye; it also gave the artists a sufficiently deep tone for the title band. C&RE repeated this trick the following year with *Natural History in the Highlands and Islands*. Unfortunately some of the subtlety of the design is lost once the jacket's spine becomes faded. Our image, taken from a proof jacket, is a reminder of what it was like originally.

The colour range of most of these 1940s designs is deliberately limited. In today's stores they might have a retro appeal, but in the austerity bookshops of postwar Britain they attracted the buyer's eye; at least 20,000 copies of *London's Natural History* were sold in 1945. Like the books themselves, these jackets were eye-catching, contemporary and rather daring.

3

London's
Natural
History

R. S. R.
FITTER

LONDON's
Natural History
R. S. R. FITTER

COLLINS

Britain's Structure & Scenery

4

L. Dudley Stamp, 1946

Britain's Structure and Scenery – or, as per the title band, 'BRITAIN's *Structure & Scenery*' – is Dudley Stamp's account of the physical structure of the British Isles. His working title, *The Build and Building of the British Isles*, provides a better sense of the book's main themes: the rocks that underlie and shape the land, and the way mankind has subsequently moulded the landscape. Dashed off in the textbook style in which he was so accomplished, Dudley Stamp's book was a great success; its use in schools, colleges and libraries made it the surprise bestseller of the series with 62,000 hardback copies sold, plus many more as Fontana paperbacks.

Structure & Scenery is densely illustrated with landscapes from a lost wartime Britain with minor roads snaking through what were then known as beauty spots without a sign or a car in sight. The artists were normally sent the first chapter and its accompanying illustrations, and the one that might have given them an idea for a jacket is Plate II, a black-and-white aerial view of the chalk coast of Dorset, with the sea stack of Old Harry rock in the foreground. C&RE's design is not Old Harry, though it is made of chalk. It is, rather, a surreal rock of their imagination which seems to metamorphose into a half-completed classical monument: 'build and building' all in one. The artists were interested in the way objects change shape when viewed from a different angle, and to this phantasmagoric rock they added a chalk cliff viewed from above which runs along the spine, with white touches indicating gulls flying up. Extraneous detail is sacrificed for a simple, strong image that says what needs to be said. And, as usual, C&RE's sense of colour is impeccable: by letting in a lot of white, the design needs no more than a cool blue, grey and buff, with overlaps to create depth and shadow.

Unlike the first three, this design was approved without modification, apart from the hand-lettered title which was changed at the last minute after Dudley Stamp had had second thoughts about *Build and Building*. The oval colophon has one of the Ellises' least successful mini-drawings, strata underlying a notional landscape, like a slice of sponge cake.

4

Britain's
Structure
and
Scenery

L.
DUDLEY
STAMP

BRITAIN's
Structure & Scenery
L. DUDLEY STAMP

COLLINS

C & R E

5   Wild Flowers

John Gilmour and Max Walters, 1954

ABOVE Colour design sketch for *Wild Flowers* in gouache and watercolour on layout paper with pencil notes (25 × 20 cm).

BELOW The original jacket for *Wild Flowers*, by John Gilmour alone and designed in 1945, was based on arrowhead lily leaves and flowers. A few copies of this jacket were printed by Baynards, but they were never used.

OPPOSITE The artwork for a new jacket (with part of the title and the imprint stuck on) was designed eight years later. C&RE also provided hand-lettered artwork for the title (see page 45), but the printed jacket substitutes machine lettering.

Wild Flowers was originally scheduled for publication in 1946, and, in that expectation, it was among the first batch of titles for which C&RE designed jackets. The then solo author, John Gilmour (he was also a member of the New Naturalist committee) had suggested two possible designs: a riverbank scene with arrowhead lilies and ragged robin or lords-and-ladies, or a woodland glade carpeted with bluebells, red campions and wild garlic. 'These three plants,' he commented, 'are very typical of many woods in late spring, and would I think make a good design.'

We discovered the artwork for the 1945 'Gilmour jacket' in the Collins archive, evidently lost for many years because it had not been catalogued. The artists had fastened on Gilmour's suggestion of the arrowhead lily, evidently admiring the bold forms of its leaves and the contrasting white, purple-centred flowers, the shape of the clubs in a pack of playing cards. Gilmour had a few criticisms: 'He feels the leaf should not bulge,' noted Ruth Atkinson. 'He is also not sure whether or not there are buds in the right-hand corner, and feels they are too large.' Gilmour and Billy Collins also thought that 'the side of the jacket is not as good as the jacket and spine seen together, and would like to have more flowers on the

WILD

COLLINS

side' (RA to CE, 26.7.45). The jacket was proofed and a copy survives to show us what the book would have looked like had it been published in 1946 instead of nearly a decade later. But Gilmour was overworked and unable to finish the book himself. It was not until he was joined by his Cambridge colleague, Max Walters, that *Wild Flowers* was completed and published in 1954. By then the series already had four botanical titles, *British Plant Life, Wild Flowers of Chalk & Limestone, Wild Orchids* and *Flowers of the Coast*, with a fifth, *Mountain Flowers*, just around the corner. Hence a new jacket was needed which C&RE were asked to make 'more striking than the original' (RT to CE, 13.3.53).

After some experiment they designed a clump of primroses framed by trees, with a lake and a green hill rising in the background. The brilliant flowers sing out from their shadowy dell as if lit by a shaft of sunshine. The design uses two yellow colours, one of them 'primrose' to match the petals of that flower as exactly as possible. At first glance the tree trunks seem to merge into the black title band, but there is in fact a subtle difference in their respective tones. The spine shows two more woodland flowers, celandine and wood anemone, along with the primrose. The design is simple, clever and striking, although some might have found it unexpectedly dark for a book about wild flowers.

RIGHT Hand-lettering and colophon for *Wild Flowers* by C&RE. By the time the book was published, they had passed out of favour.

Wild Flowers

45

6 Natural History in the Highlands and Islands

F. Fraser Darling, 1947

Revised and renamed the Highlands & Islands by F. Fraser Darling and Morton Boyd, 1964.

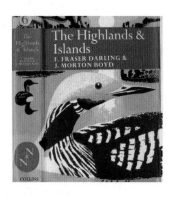

ABOVE The jacket of the revised edition published in 1964 and retitled *The Highlands & Islands*, differs in various details, most notably in the absence of the antler on the colophon.

Many of the New Naturalist jackets designed in the immediate postwar period depend on a single bright colour among soft, subdued tones. The powerful jacket of *Natural History in the Highlands and Islands* is a good example. The artists chose a Black-throated Diver as a suitable living symbol of the wild and solitary spaces of northern Scotland. The bird's strange appearance and black-and-white plumage also made it a striking subject. Having made the diver fill most of the available space, its head turned back in the same manner as the partridge on *British Game*, the rest of the design could be sketched in. There is no detail, only blotchy browns and dark greys suggesting rocks, and the lighter tones the light shimmering over the water. No more is necessary. The diver carries all before it. *Simplex munditiis* ('elegant in simplicity').

The use of colour on this jacket is confident to the point of bravery. With everything else in black, grey and bistre-brown, C&RE confined the only solid bright colour, a biologically accurate maroon, to the diver's eye, which lies at the exact optical centre of the jacket. A delicate stippling of the maroon ink forms a pinkish flush on the diver's chin. Its mate, reflected in the still water, paddles on the spine, above the oval containing a stag's antler.

For the 1964 revised edition the book was given a new title, *The Highlands & Islands* (by Darling and Boyd). The jacket of the new edition is brighter overall and the bird's head paler due to the substitution of buff for grey. And on the oval, the stag's antler has 'gang awa'.

6

Natural History in the Highlands and Islands

F. FRASER DARLING

Natural
History
in the
Highlands
and
Islands

F. FRASER
DARLING

Natural History in the Highlands and Islands

F. FRASER DARLING

COLLINS

Mushrooms & Toadstools

7

John Ramsbottom, 1953

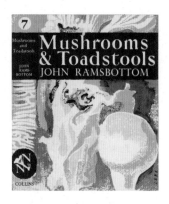

ABOVE Pencil study of
mushroom gills used as the
basis of the spine of the jacket.

OPPOSITE Artwork for
Mushrooms & Toadstools in four
colours with pencilled printing
instructions and marks where it
had been gummed to the plate.

This is one of C&RE's more experimental designs. Clifford had made a series of
pencil studies of mushrooms, puffballs and other fungi, and he and Rosemary
chose some of these to combine into a collage of textures and tones. The result is
a kind of essence of 'fungosity', with the wavy and swirling shapes of fungal gills
contrasted with the bulging form of a puffball and the indented stem of a False
Morel, *Helvella crispa*. The artists decided against projecting the design on to the
spine, finding it more effective to reproduce a mushroom's gills to provide a
suitably fungussy effect.

Both publishers and author were pleased with the design which, they thought,
caught 'the atmosphere of the book'. The main concern was the date of 1945 in the
lower right-hand corner. C&RE had designed it in that year when publication had
seemed imminent. But no one had allowed for the author John Ramsbottom's
seemingly unlimited aptitude for procrastination. His impossibly long text had
to be pruned right down, and then, at the last minute, the editors asked him to
write an extra chapter about penicillin. Hence, like *Wild Flowers*, this book came
out eight years after the date on the jacket. This was the reason why the artists were
asked not to date their designs in future.

As usual, the jacket was printed by lithography at Baynard Press. Jackets for later
editions of this long-running title were printed on whiter paper. When it came to
the last reprint, in 1977, the original artwork could not be found, and so the printer
quietly photographed an old jacket and hoped for the best. The result was a travesty.

That year C&RE designed a brand-new, more colourful jacket for the book with
puffballs and magpie caps on a slightly surreal pink background. This was one of
the few jackets Charlotte Ellis remembered seeing in preparation, with fresh-
gathered magpie caps laid out on paper ready to draw. Sadly the new jacket was
never printed; instead, the book, like so many other classic titles, was allowed to
go out of print.

7

New Naturalist

MUSHROOMS & TOADSTOOLS

4 colours printed in following order

CRE '45

8 Insect Natural History

A. D. Imms, 1947

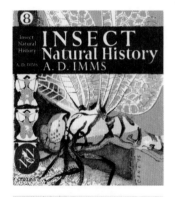

The striking jacket of *Insect Natural History* was designed in late 1945. Because this book would largely omit butterflies and moths to focus on less well-known insects, C&RE chose instead a dragonfly. The Ellises were clearly fascinated by the textures of an adult dragonfly, the veined wings, like leaded glass, the intricate exoskeleton, the bristly legs and the huge bulging eyes. A large pencil drawing offers some insight into the way the jacket was designed. Over it, Clifford had ruled intersecting square and diagonal lines probably for the purposes of transposing the design to the size of the printed jacket. He also added many pencilled annotations for the colours: the abdominal segments were to be 'pale green'; other parts sepia, chrome or 'soft edged as seen through gelatin'. The wings were to be 'slightly paler and lighter but not white'. A second colour sketch on thick watercolour paper tries out the effect of the colours, and both would be used to guide the completed artwork.

The printed jacket is a showcase of visual effects: the marbling of the rock, the interplay of reflected light on the wings, the refracted shine on the dragonfly's eye. A close-up of three more abdominal plates, seen from a different angle, make up the spine, one of them enclosing the oval which contains not another dragonfly but a grasshopper. The title is exquisitely hand-lettered.

Insect Natural History was among the second batch of jacket designs sent to Collins on 9 October 1945. 'The New Naturalist committee have now seen the jackets', wrote Ruth Atkinson, 'and I am told like them very much indeed. So does everyone else. I am delighted with them and feel very god-motherly about them' (RA to CE, 9.8.45).

Nearly a quarter century later, after the original 'plant' for the jacket had been lost, C&RE were asked to design another for an expected new edition, which they completed by October 1979. Unfortunately the book was not reprinted and so the new jacket, now seemingly lost, was never used.

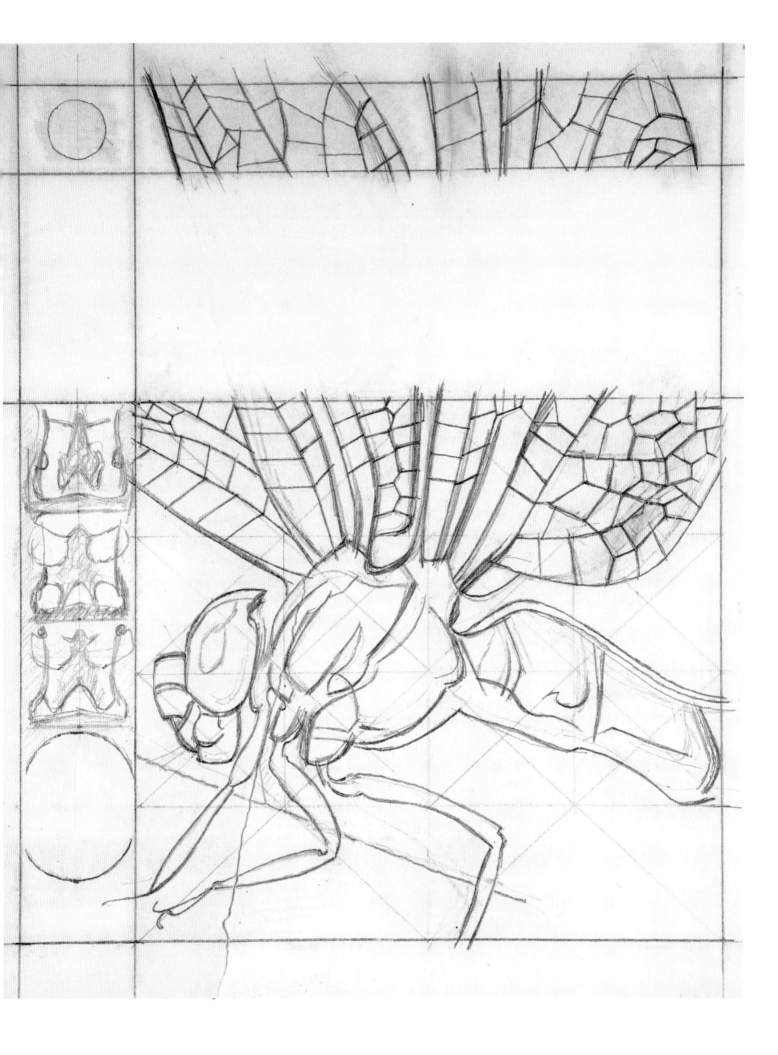

9 A Country Parish

A. W. Boyd, 1951

A Country Parish was the New Naturalist library's tribute to *The Natural History of Selborne*. Like its great predecessor, it combined natural history with accounts of the physical and historical aspects of the parish, together with short digressions about village characters, local dialect and quaint customs. Written in the 1940s it can be read now as a portrait of a rural village before cars, television and supermarkets swept away many of the age-old rustic traditions of country life.

The problem for the jacket was how to convey the idea of a parish. While only a map could show us what a parish is, C&RE found an appropriate symbol for a village community on the very first of the book's 32 colour plates: Great Budworth church with its brass weathervane. The church lies at the heart, physically and spiritually, of a parish, where swifts often nest in the eaves and bats hang in the rafters. The weathervane on the church tower or spire is an even more effective symbol for a book about natural history because it unites the parish with the physical elements of wind and weather. C&RE's weathercock is a strange thing, stained and covered in green verdigris, aloft amid a whirly-go-round of swallows: a man-made bird among real ones. This is a sky scene rendered in appropriately cool dove-greys and lavenders. A contrasting blue-green band bearing the hand-lettered title completes the design.

This was perhaps the most unusual design so far, and seems to have come as a surprise. Ruth Atkinson's reaction was, 'Yes, but … The idea is fresh, so needs imagination.' It is also one of the least familiar – *A Country Parish* went out of print towards the end of the 1950s and has never been reprinted.

10   British Plant Life

W. B. Turrill, 1948

The choice of a sea-cliff setting for this jacket might seem an odd one considering that *Flowers of the Coast* and *The Sea Coast* were both in active preparation and had a better claim to it. The choice was not the artists' but the publishers'. 'It has been decided that the plant to be depicted is Sea Campion on shingle or cliff,' wrote Ruth Atkinson (RA to CE, 7.10.46). The book's author, W. B. Turrill, had written a book about the Bladder Campion and its close relative, the Sea Campion, and his work on their ecology, cytology and genetics features strongly in the text. Clearly Turrill wanted the jacket to reflect that fact. *British Plant Life* embodied the new botany of the postwar era, no longer dominated by classification and plant anatomy but reaching into the uncharted waters of microbiology and the light it shed on plant relationships. As the editors expressed it, such work was 'a signpost pointing towards a fuller and deeper knowledge of our flora and we hope that many will be encouraged to follow the road to which it points.'

For this unusually tight brief, C&RE designed a cliff scene, probably because it suited a vertical format better than a beach or shingle bank. A headland resembling The Needles in the Isle of Wight made a satisfying composition, leaving the flowers to dominate the foreground, with one of them leaning over onto the spine. The campions are carefully and accurately drawn with delicately veined calyces, dark stamens and paired waxy leaves. The colours are soft and cool: mauve, blue-green and pale grey, using overlaps for the shadows. C&RE chose a contrasting plant for the oval, a frond of Hart's-tongue Fern.

British
Plant
Life

W. B.
TURRILL

British Plant Life
W. B. TURRILL

COLLINS

Mountains & Moorlands

I I

W. H. Pearsall, 1950

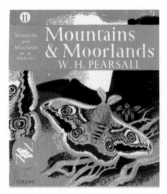

OPPOSITE Artwork for
Mountains & Moorlands with part
of Clifford Ellis's instructions for
printers added in pencil.

The *Mountains & Moorlands* jacket was among a batch commissioned in late 1946, and completed early the following year. It is notable both for its stark and tangled shapes and the choice of colours – subdued greys and ochre-oranges with a sparing use of the same bright magenta as in *The Highlands and Islands.* James Fisher considered it to be a particularly beautiful design but was intrigued by the choice of a moth to represent the wilder British uplands. Was there 'a special reason for choosing a moth?' asked a member of the Collins team, Constance Yates. Clifford's reply does not survive, but read on.

Tim Bernhard is a graphic designer, wildlife artist and book collector who currently runs the New Naturalists Collectors Club. *Mountains & Moorlands* was the first jacketed New Naturalist he came to own, and it sowed the seeds of his passion for wildlife art. He writes:

'This is a four-colour design. There is a lovely bright golden-ochre which features on the title band and the spine, and also on the body and wings of the Emperor moth. A sort of olive-greenish-grey is used for the sky and foreground. Then there is black, which brings the design into focus, and introduces power and depth. And finally there is a rich, deep magenta which, when printed over the black, softens and warms the landscape. It is also used to great effect on the wings of the moth, the bell heather flowers and the book number.

A second Emperor moth on the spine is more abstract than its mate on the cover, but retains enough detail to be recognisable; I love the use of the same moth for the colophon. I have lived with this jacket for thirty years, and I am still impressed by C&RE's bleak, harsh landscape, a desolate moor just before a storm, with the strong, twisting branches of the heather giving movement and vitality to the design. By contrast the moths are soft and textured with downy fur and velvety markings. It is a striking, unexpected and rather moving interpretation of a vulnerable creature in a harsh environment, and it is not only one of my favourite New Naturalist covers but, in my opinion, one of the best book jackets there has ever been.'

C&RE

The Sea Shore

12

C. M. Yonge, 1949

C&RE's original design for *The Sea Shore* used a khaki tone to suggest a beach on which a crab's claw lies bleaching and half-buried in the sand. They were not satisfied with it and tried another version substituting greyish-green for khaki which made a better contrast with the pink of the claw and suggested a rock encrusted with barnacles and limpets. The artists clearly had fun with the shapes and textures of the image, and the result is arresting, the grittiness of the background suggested by blotches of black and white, thus focusing attention on that massive claw. The spine shows another crab fragment, the paddle-like hind-leg of a swimming crab.

The Sea Shore, like most of the early jackets, was first printed by lithography, and later by letterpress. The design, along with that of *The Badger*, was included in a National Book League Exhibition of British book jackets at the Victoria and Albert Museum in 1949. Many other Ellis jackets were similarly exhibited in future years.

Nick Baker, the naturalist and broadcaster, writes:

'This design is one of my favourites, partly because the subject strikes me as a little dark and disturbing. To see one of the book's subjects dismembered on the front cover is in itself a little unusual: imagine, if you will, what the jacket of *Dragonflies* might look like with the shattered panes and torn panels of its wings, the post-predation wreckage caused by a spider or bird (actually I quite like this idea now I've thought about it!), or the disjointed and mangled limbs of the rabbit on *British Mammals*. Yet for some reason it was fine to have bits of crab scattered hither and thither on the jacket of *The Sea Shore* by C. M. Yonge. Whether this is a maimed or simply a moulted crab doesn't really matter. The jacket did the trick for me, as a proto-naturalist on a family holiday to the Isle of Wight, when finding the distinctive hind-leg of a Velvet Crab drew my eye to the spine of The Sea Shore in a secondhand bookshop in Ventnor. The image encapsulated for me the mysteries of the shore that I was exploring daily, the hardships of this harsh environment, and, of course, the trail of delight for any naturalist who visits the shore.'

The Sea Shore

The Sea Shore

C. M. YONGE

C. M. YONGE

COLLINS

I3

Snowdonia The National Park of North Wales

F. J. North, Bruce Campbell and Richenda Scott, 1949

Snowdonia was among a planned series of 'regional' titles on the newly opened National Parks and other areas of distinctive scenery rich in wildlife. In each case the plan was for a team of experts, under a senior editor, to contribute sections of the book from their specialised viewpoints, mixing natural history with land use, rocks and landforms, and cultural life to produce a composite portrait of a region. In practice this was far too ambitious; none of the published titles fully realise that concept, and some were never completed. *Snowdonia* is the closest the series came to the original conception. Though it is subtitled 'The National Park of North Wales', the book was published before the Park was declared and its boundaries agreed: a somewhat hazardous proceeding.

William Collins wanted the regional books to 'look different from the New Naturalists and yet be enough alike for people to have some linked feeling.' A photographic jacket was considered but, for the moment, rejected (it would raise its ugly head again in the 1960s). Instead, the Ellises were asked to produce something akin to a travel poster, a landscape simplified into its basic geometry and reproducible in a limited range of colours.

The jacket shows an elemental scene of rock, snow and water without relieving detail. Windswept boulders and snow mark the steep ascent above a mountain lake. The deep-blue of the mountain lake is matched by a stormy sky, while crags and hollows are suggested in soft greys. This is probably intended to be a view of Snowdon itself, with the llyn or lake of Glaslyn lying below its distinctively domed summit. The title band is narrower than usual and is not coloured. The colophon is a National Trust-style oak leaf. The design was completed by January 1947 and was well-received. C&RE were, however, asked not to date the jackets in future, since the book was published in November 1949, and not in 1947 as on the jacket.

Perhaps because the book lacks a senior editor (it is really three separate books in one) the jacket omits the authors' names. Their names appear on the binding of some copies but not on others.

13

SNOWDONIA

SNOWDONIA
The National Park of North Wales

COLLINS

14 The Art of Botanical Illustration

Wilfrid Blunt, 1950

To the regret of New Naturalist collectors ever since, *The Art of Botanical Illustration* was denied an Ellis jacket. The plain colophon was designed by C&RE but the rest of the jacket did not involve them. The Board minutes state baldly that an Ellis wrapper 'would not be suitable for this book'. It seems that the decision was taken internally and was not up for discussion. As a result, although everything else, from the binding to the paper quality, is in the usual New Naturalist style, the jacket gives this book a semi-detached look.

In place of the usual design is a framed print taken from the book, a painting of roses by Johann Walther of Strasbourg within a buff background (the original is in the Victoria and Albert Museum). The spine makes do with a drawing of a lily by R. G. Hatton inside an oval; the delicate buff tone tends to deepen over time to an unpleasing burnt umber.

The Art of
Botanical Illustration

WILFRID BLUNT

COLLINS

15 Life in Lakes & Rivers

T. T. Macan and E. B. Worthington, 1951

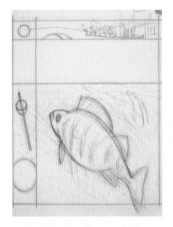

<small>ABOVE Full size pencil design for *Life in Lakes & Rivers* on layout paper and the published jacket.</small>

<small>OPPOSITE Artwork for *Life in Lakes & Rivers* in four colours with part of printers' instructions. The pencil line around the perch was added by the printers.</small>

One of the authors, T. T. Macan, had some very specific suggestions for the jacket of what was then called *Britain's Lakes and Rivers*. He asked for 'an impression of a lake in section, with a fish in it, and an insect or two, and a fisherman above, and perhaps a factory menacing in the background, and some plants, and some reeds' (conveyed to CE by Ruth Atkinson, 15.12.48). C&RE kept surprisingly close to the spirit, if not the letter, of this daunting brief.

They had an idea of their own to offer. The book's themes of freshwater life and man's impact on this environment could be linked by a fish and a fisherman. But rather than revealing the fisherman himself, it would be sufficient to show part of his tackle, in this case a float. And the title band could divide the watery world of fish from the man's-eye view of the river with its road bridge and tumbling weir. The various elements that Macan suggested are thus integrated nicely in one of the most imaginative of the Ellis designs.

But it created a technical problem. The design called for two shades of green with which darker tones could be made by overlapping them with grey. Baynard Press experienced difficulty getting the colours exactly right, though in the end they obtained a passable result by adjusting the grey, which appears as a pure tone only on the bridge. At some point the printers traced a pencil line around the perch on the artwork. In a note which betrays the casualness with which C&RE's original artwork was treated, the editor claimed the jacket of a later edition of the book was an improvement: 'You will notice how much nearer the blockmaker has got to the original'. The artwork could be found 'with the other NN wrappers held by your department in the dusty alcove above the plastic curtain in your room'.

4 colours
in following
order of printing

① Grey — as in index ③ Yellow Green, an

C&RE

16 Wild Flowers of Chalk & Limestone

J. E. Lousley, 1950

The jacket of this book sought to combine wild flowers with their hillside habitat. The author, Ted Lousley, had suggested a scene of 'rolling downs and a chalk face' with a selection of wild flowers in the foreground (RT to CE, 23.6.49). Clifford Ellis made several pencil sketches on the margin of the letter conveying that idea to him, perhaps just moments after reading it. By coincidence, and around the same time, Victor Summerhayes, the author of *Wild Orchids of Britain*, had made a similar suggestion for his own book: an 'Early Purple Orchid against a background of limestone slopes or downland'. Both ideas found their way on to Lousley's book, but with a twist.

C&RE discovered a more arresting way of suggesting a 'chalk face' by including the Westbury White Horse on the Wiltshire Downs. On the spine they added a second iconic image of the downs: a clump of beech trees crowning a hill. For the wild flowers, they chose a single species, the Early Purple Orchid, probably for the vivid contrast it offered of magenta against bright green (a third colour, the artists' favourite pale grey, was used mainly for overlaps). This particular orchid is normally a woodland species that does not grow in the open on chalk downs (though it does on the limestone dales of northern England), but perhaps botanical literalism is beside the point. But it was a pity, as Billy Collins pointed out, that they had chosen an orchid, since they could hardly avoid designing another orchid jacket for Summerhayes' book.

Though it was printed in three colours, this is a bright and cheerful jacket to match an open-air sort of book. Yet the business of transforming artwork into a printed jacket was far from cheerful. The cost of colour printing had risen enormously since the war. One sign of this was the diminution of colour plates in some of the latest New Naturalist titles from 32 or 48 to 16, 8 or even fewer. Collins were anxious to find less expensive methods to produce the jackets, and the obvious way was to print them in-house.

Wild Flowers of Chalk & Limestone became the subject of experiments designed to make this possible. But the Collins factory in Glasgow was used to printing colours using screens, which would subdue the bright colours of the New Naturalist jackets and weaken their effect. To avoid this, the factory supplied the artists with plastic transparencies and Bristol Board for producing 'colour separations' which the printers would combine on the plate with a camera. The artists used both materials but the proof was disappointing, the red losing its intended richness and the dark green coming out as nearly black. The second proof was equally poor with the black (used for the orchids' pollen-bearing organs) hardly showing at all (RT to CE, 7.7.50).

All of this proved to be extremely time-consuming for a jacket that was needed urgently. The experiments were written off as a failure, and the publishers abandoned colour separations for the time being (with the exception of two titles, *The Greenshank* and *An Angler's Entomology*). In the end, the jacket of *Wild Flowers of Chalk & Limestone* was produced from scratch by the tried-and-tested method, probably by Baynard Press. The first edition was printed on creamy paper. The 1969 reprint is on whiter paper, which the Collins editor considered an improvement.

17 Birds & Men

E. M. Nicholson, 1951

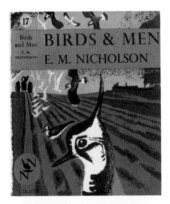

OPPOSITE Alternative design for *Birds & Men* showing a thrush on a snowy path with a snowman on the spine. Full size, gouache and pencil notes on watercolour paper.

ABOVE Colour sketch for revised design, approximately half the size of the printed jacket.

Like the previous jacket, that of *Birds & Men* was caught up in Collins' ill-fated cost-cutting experiments. Hence its production was prolonged. The artists, it seems, made three designs. One was, until recently, thought to be an alternative design for the later title, *Man & Birds*. This was apparently considered 'too popular'. Another, which showed a flock of gulls following a tractor, was thought too similar to the jacket of *London's Natural History*. However, the basic idea was considered sound, so the artists agreed to redraw it, substituting lapwings for some of the gulls and shifting the tractor to the book's spine. A close-up lapwing gave the jacket its needed impact. It was a felicitous choice: in the 1930s the book's author, Max Nicholson, had organised the first nationwide survey of this bird.

This is not a pretty jacket. The furrowed earth was printed in heavy tones of brown, and the farm, with its wind-blasted trees beneath a brooding lavender sky, looks desolate and uncomfortable. To try to cut the mounting costs of book production, Baynard Press had suggested that C&RE should draw directly on to the printing plates. The results, however, were so unsatisfactory that Billy Collins ruled that the work should be redone 'in the usual way' (Patricia Cohen to CE, 17.7.50).

The cost-cutting expedients for this jacket and *Wild Flowers of Chalk & Limestone* had created considerable work for the artists without any improvement in quality. 'My quarrel with the proof was that chalk work and small detail generally had become much coarser in the proof,' complained Clifford. 'It may be the moment to drop a hint that the whole business is on the point of becoming a bore. Each design calls for first-hand research, and, as often as not, long journeys, although the final selection of material suitable for a jacket may give little indication of what has been discarded. There is therefore little financial advantage in doing the jobs at all and the unsatisfactory handling of the reproduction at the end of it all is discouraging' (CE to RT, 3.8.50). An apologetic letter from Collins soon arrived with the promise that they did 'not intend to do any more experimenting with methods of reproduction' (RT to CE, 3.8.50).

Brown

C & R E

Title, Author & Colophon in White

N' "Birds & Man"

18

A Natural History of Man in Britain

H. J. Fleure, 1951

The rather sombre jacket of *A Natural History of Man in Britain* was the fruit of a fascinating correspondence between Clifford Ellis and the book's author, the elderly Professor Fleure. The latter had suggested 'a hillfort rising like an island above wooded slopes'. While that idea held some promise, Fleure went on to propose a man or two as well, perhaps as sentries guarding the fort. Clifford Ellis replied with a patient explanation of the difference between a jacket design and an illustration:

'I will begin, I hope not too impertinently, by saying something of book jackets. A book jacket is by way of being a small poster: it is part of the machinery of book selling. Though, obviously enough, the jacket should be in keeping with the book it contains, it is unwise to consider it as an opportunity for an additional illustration. An illustration, as against the jacket, can be seen at leisure, and free from the competition of not always very mannerly neighbours. The jacket should be immediately interesting; its forms and colours should make a very clear and distinctive image. If it does its job the book will be taken down and opened, and the proper illustrations will be seen. We suggest, therefore, that the hill fort should be seen from the air. Though one would lose the sentries, who would be too small to show, one would gain a more striking view of the earthworks and (speaking now as a sometime Camouflage Officer) there would be a remarkable colour contrast between the smooth grass of the hill and the dark tree foliage of its surroundings. If you agree to this suggestion, have you a preference for any one fort? Is Maiden Castle too unusual, or too well-known? If you cared to lend us air photographs, we would take great care of them and return them within a few days' (CE to Professor Fleure, undated 1948).

Fleure agreed, proposing a couple of earthworks. He also suggested autumn colours to mark All Souls' Day, November 2nd, one of 'the two outstanding dates of the prehistoric calendar'. C&RE decided to combine the white horse with an aerial view of a chalk hill and the distant fields beyond beneath a dark late-autumn sky. A chalk track winding up the hill enlivens an otherwise unusually bare spine.

A Natural
History
of Man
in Britain

H. J.
FLEURE

A Natural History
of Man in Britain

H. J. FLEURE

COLLINS

19

Wild Orchids of Britain

V. S. Summerhayes, 1951

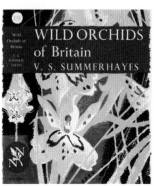

TOP Colour sketch with pencil notes for alternative design on layout paper, approximately half the size of the printed jacket (above).

OPPOSITE Detail from a pencil study of Bee Orchid with notes (32 × 20.3 cm).

Fate seemed to treat *Wild Orchids* and *Wild Flowers of Chalk & Limestone* the same. They were published and reprinted at about the same time and many of their lavish colour illustrations, among the best in the series so far, were by the same man, Robert Atkinson. And, as chance had defined it, both had a wild orchid on the jacket.

Perhaps in an effort to depart as far as possible from the *Chalk & Limestone* jacket, C&RE decided to base this jacket on a bee orchid, with its strange, insect-like flowers. A pencil drawing (opposite) survives of a bee orchid spotted by Clifford on the North Walk at Corsham Court. Against the drawing he made detailed notes of the anatomy and exact colours of the flower for working up into a jacket design. All that survives of the bee orchid jacket is a colour sketch based on a close-up of the flower in pink, brown and greeny-yellow against a backcloth of grass blades. The bulging lip of a second bee orchid runs down the spine. It would have made an eye-catching jacket, yet the editors did not take to it, objecting that the public might mistake it for a real bee! It would be better, they said, 'if the artists chose another orchid which has a sensational shape and beautiful colour, but which bears no resemblance to an animal' (James Fisher, file note, c. March 1951).

Patiently the Ellises worked on a second design based on the more conventional-looking flowers of the Common Spotted Orchid. The flowers have bold shapes and interesting markings, and their pale colours made a nice contrast with the fresh green used for the grass blades. The least successful aspect of the new design was the spine. Perhaps because they did not want to repeat the separated flowers on the spine of *Chalk and Limestone*, they attempted to show the whole orchid spike, but the result, especially when the spine has faded, looks like candyfloss and doesn't really work.

The jacket of the 1968 revised edition was printed on whiter paper which gives a fresher appearance though perhaps lacking some of the subtlety of the original.

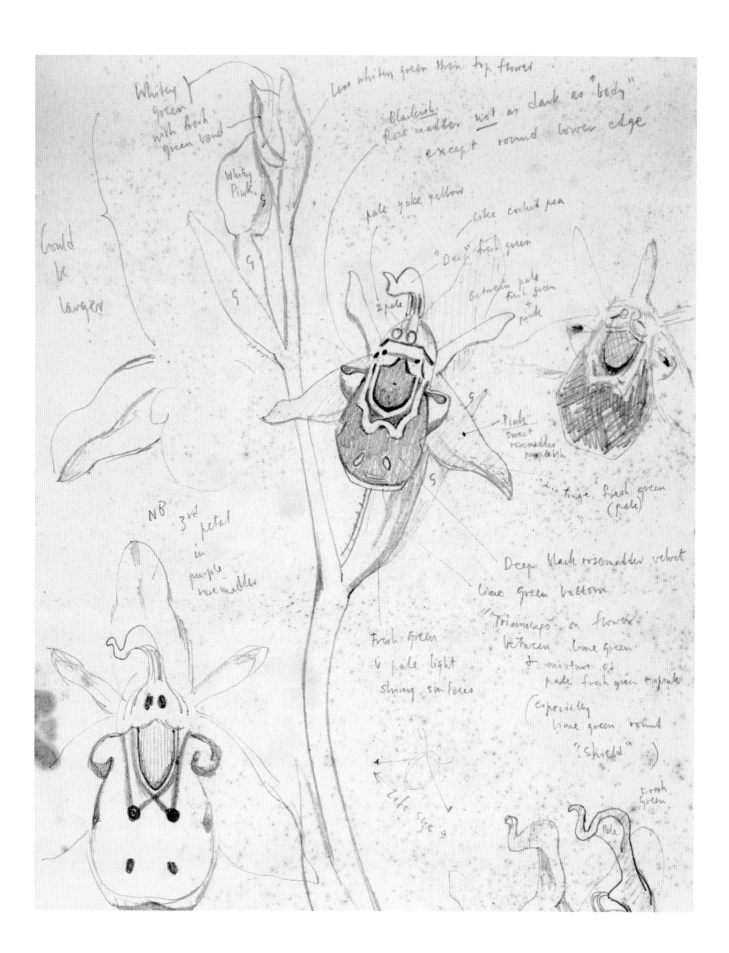

Whity green with fresh green bond

Less whiten green than top flower

Blackish Rose madder not as dark as "body" except round lower edge

Whity Pink. 5

pale yoke yellow

like cooked pea

"Deep" fresh green

Between pale fresh green + pink

2 pale

Could be larger

5

5

Pink sweet rosemadder purplish

5

5

... tinge fresh green (pale)

NB 3rd petal in purple rosemadder

Deep black rosemadder velvet

Lime green bottom

"Triangles" on flower between lime green + mixture of pale fresh green + pink

Fresh green & pale light shiny surfaces

(especially lime green round "Shield")

like egg

Fresh green

Pale

20 The British Amphibians and Reptiles

Malcolm Smith, 1951

This, perhaps most people would agree, is a lovely design. The snake seems to come to life as it slithers through the grass blades, the head at the top of the spine, and its body coiling down the spine and over the front to rest in the register above the title band. The adder's zigzag pattern is a perfect match for the flashes of tawny grass. It is C&RE at their best: simple, bold, satisfying, and saying all that needs to be said.

Yet the author of the book, the veteran herpetologist Malcolm Smith, was not happy with it. 'The colours are all wrong,' he complained. 'There is no pure white on the adder nor have I ever seen one with the colour of No. 2 [yellow-brown]. I suggest that the white be made deep cream and that No. 2 be replaced by No. 3 [deep brick-red]' (conveyed to CE by RT, 9.12.49). Smith had asked for a frog on the jacket and was perhaps miffed to find an adder instead.

Raleigh Trevelyan passed on these remarks to Clifford, adding his own opinion that 'it would be a pity to take out the white on the snake, as it lends so much to the design …' Clifford replied on a postcard:

'We are aware that adders are not white, but new-sloughed they gleam in the sun. Our problem was to find something that would gleam in a bookshop and could be printed in four colours. N.B. This raises the whole problem of inviting authors' ideas for wrappers. We would much prefer to have a synopsis of the book. If you want to keep down the costs of colour printing and have something that reads well in the bookshop, the designer must have a wide field of subject matter from which to select. We for our part would try to catch the spirit of the book and to be as "accurate" as circumstances permitted. But our idea of "accuracy" is to base our design on first-hand experience of the subject – selecting such aspects of it as are appropriate and possible for the job – but it is not our intention to make a coloured diagram, nor is this a practical possibility in four colours' (CE to RT, 1.1.50).

Trevelyan wrote to Clifford: 'I have told the New Naturalist [*sic*] that any suggestions we get from the authors for designs of the wrappers are to be suggestions only, to be used by you should you find them helpful' (RT to CE, 11.1.50).

20

The
British
Amphibians
and
Reptiles

MALCOLM
SMITH

The British Amphibians
and Reptiles
MALCOLM SMITH

COLLINS

C & R E

British Mammals

L. Harrison Matthews, 1952

It might have been tricky to design an original jacket for *British Mammals* when so many of them – seals, squirrels, moles, badgers, red deer, bats – were commissioned subjects for New Naturalist monographs. The process was, in fact, unusually protracted, and was not helped by printing economies pressed on C&RE by the editors. Their first design was of a stag's head, in red-brown, grey and green, but it was thought to resemble the colours of *Birds and Men* too closely, and the stag had 'almost too weird an effect' (RT to CE, 4.9.50).

The fox and the rabbit of the published jacket now made their entrance, but the original fox was shown much nearer and its head peered round the spine. The rabbit, by contrast, was crouched down and hard to recognise. The jacket was seen as 'very sombre' with 'too much black in the middle of the design' (RT to CE, 21.2.51). Nor did the editor like their treatment of some leaves which 'merge too much into the background' while the rabbit 'does not look like a rabbit until you look at the design carefully'. Could it be made to sit up more?

For their third design, the Ellises retained the theme of the hunter-fox and the hunted-rabbit but consigned the fox to the background and removed the vegetation. The colours are economical – a cold blue-green and two greys ('It was a great saving for us that you managed to do the *Mammals* design in only three colours,' exclaimed the cost-conscious editor). The rabbit is alert but motionless, hoping it hasn't been spotted. But it has. A fox's eyes reflect green in lamp light, and they have a mirror-like retina, the tapetum, which helps it to see in the dark. It is these eerie mirrors within the slim silhouette of the light-footed fox that lend this jacket its sense of chill. Within an austere design, the artists convey a number of key aspects of the book – the hunter and the hunted, shadowy shapes in the dark, and the tense intelligence on display as one animal tries to outwit the other.

Stefan Buczacki, the author, broadcaster and naturalist-gardener – and author of New Naturalist 102, *Garden Natural History* – writes:

'The eyes have it. The *British Mammals* jacket is certainly all about eyes, and it was the possibility that there might be triocular creatures wandering the British countryside that first attracted me to it. The three-eyed rabbit on the spine and its one-eyed companion on the front, where it is spotted by the staring, blank-faced two-eyed fox, are compelling and almost fantastical images. Their hypnotic attraction was enhanced because this was the volume whose spine stared down at me from the natural history shelves of the school library where I spent many a lunch time. Those eyes had me hooked, and for someone whose primary passion had long been for cold-blooded rather than warm-blooded creatures, they all but converted me to the warm and furry. Today, nearly half a century later, I simply cannot think of British mammals of any kind without those riveting three eyes returning to haunt me. In truth, the three-eyed spine doesn't immediately say 'mammals', but then how many other New Naturalist spines really spell out the book's contents? For me, their cleverness lies in their ability to tempt you to withdraw the volume from the shelf and discover more; both about the rest of the jacket and, of course, the text. But even for artists whose special appeal was largely born of their economy of style and colour, the Ellis jacket to Volume 21 is design stripped practically bare, and is fabulous for that – almost literally so.'

Climate and the British Scene

Gordon Manley, 1952

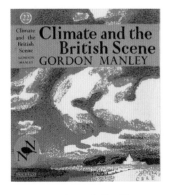

OPPOSITE Artwork for *Climate and the British Scene* with pencilled instructions by Clifford Ellis.

One is struck sometimes by the contrast between C&RE's sympathetic, even affectionate, depiction of animals, and the harshness of so many of their landscapes: the dark, barren hills of *Mountains & Moorlands*, the angry sky and weather-blasted farm of *Birds & Men*, or the gloomy chasm that bisects the jacket of *The Peak District*. For the jacket of *Climate and the British Scene*, the weather book of the series, Gordon Manley, had suggested 'sky and cumulus clouds, giving the suggestion of changeable weather, with typical scenery included' (conveyed to CE in 8.47). The Ellises obliged, but theirs is not a sky anyone would want to picnic under. Clouds edged with grey dwarf the darkened landscape. One, the shape of a flexed arm, threatens the lonely church as if about to crush it with its cloudy fist. The air is speckled with black and white as though the mother of all thunderstorms is taking shape. The overall sense is of the fragility of human pretensions when faced with the majestic power of nature. But there is one redeeming note: a little bird, puffed up against the cold, snug inside the colophon.

The artwork for *Climate and the British Scene* used chalk and delicate brushwork on top of three cold colours, blue, moss-green and pale grey (plus black), to achieve its effect. The design, with its hand-lettered title, was completed in 1947, well in advance of the book; if the New Naturalists were arranged in the order in which the jackets were designed, this one would weigh in at about number 12!

numerals
in
WHITE

C&RE

printed in following order

① Green

② Grey

23

An Angler's Entomology

J. R. Harris, 1952

ABOVE Study of a mayfly for the jacket of *An Angler's Entomology*. Pencil with notes on bond-type paper.

James Fisher regarded angler-naturalists as 'one of the pillars of British natural history'. He hoped that the series could include a book written by a fisherman about entomology, or alternatively a book about angling written by an entomologist. By happy chance, an author who was both an angler and an entomologist, J. R. Harris of Trinity College Dublin, contacted Collins to say he was interested in writing such a book, and, moreover, he knew an expert photographer who could produce reasonable colour images of mayflies.

The jacket of *An Angler's Entomology* was produced in 1949, three years ahead of publication. C&RE adopted James Fisher's suggestion of 'a mayfly and a lure mayfly' (i.e. an insect and its artificial fishing-fly counterpart). Using only three colours, pale brown, blue-grey and black, their design shows a monstrous mayfly – a mature adult known as a spinner – dancing above the water. The image is almost free from extraneous detail, with cross-hatching to create extra tone in the shadows. The background is simply suggested above the title band. The mayfly's fishing-fly counterpart is wrapped around the spine and displays the sharpest feature of the design, the black tie-wires and hook, with three artificial tail streamers projecting through the oval.

Julian Huxley and James Fisher liked the design (which they had shown to 'various fishermen') but found the image of the mayfly rather insubstantial. But the semi-translucent effect may have been deliberate: mayflies are ephemeral, fairy-like insects, and the artists brought out their combination of grace and insect legginess, the pulpy, spotted abdomen contrasted with the ephemeral shining wings.

This jacket was the only success in a series of otherwise disappointing printing experiments. The blocks were made using C&RE's colour separations by Odhams of Watford, and the jacket was printed either by Odhams or Collins. Clifford persuaded the publishers to stump up a little extra cash to print the design on good-quality white paper to emphasise the gleam in the mayfly's wing. This was one of Rosemary's favourite jackets.

An Angler's Entomology

J. R. HARRIS

COLLINS

24 Flowers of the Coast

Ian Hepburn, 1952

This jacket is one of the few that could be labelled a failure. The fault lay not in the design but in the printing. Its centrepiece is a pink Sea Bindweed flower, which makes a strong and satisfying shape around which the other elements – vegetation, dunes, a distant lighthouse – can be fitted. On the spine sits a second bindweed flower with its petals furled like an umbrella inside a heart-shaped sepal. But the effect depended on printing the three colours, pink, blue and yellow, in the right order, and using exact tones to create extra colours, most notably green. Unfortunately this jacket was among the first to be produced by the new blockmakers at Odhams. Try as they might, they could not prevent the intended green from appearing as a muddy shade of blue, while cliff-top, sea and sky merged into a pink-flecked smog.

'The colour process for the jacket is unfortunately only partially mechanical', wrote Clifford, 'and for the rest it is far from fool-proof. The blocks themselves are good – we give bad marks only for the ineffective filtering of the sky in the block. But the honest-to-goodness ability to mix and match a colour, and especially the tone of a colour, is lacking. When, as in this design, we have tried to do with 3 colours what used to be done with 4, it is imperative that the exact colours of the original should be matched. Both blue and yellow are far too weak … If it really worries you, have white let in round the leaf – but only on the blue block, and as we have indicated, there, NOT as the mechanical line the blockmaker has so very improperly added to the original' (CE to RT, 9.4.52). Odhams replied that they were confident they could do better next time.

Flowers of the Coast marked the last appearance of the charming individual colophons the artists had designed for each title since 1945. 'We have decided that it would probably be best to have a general New Naturalist colophon instead,' wrote Raleigh Trevelyan, shortly, and without further explanation.

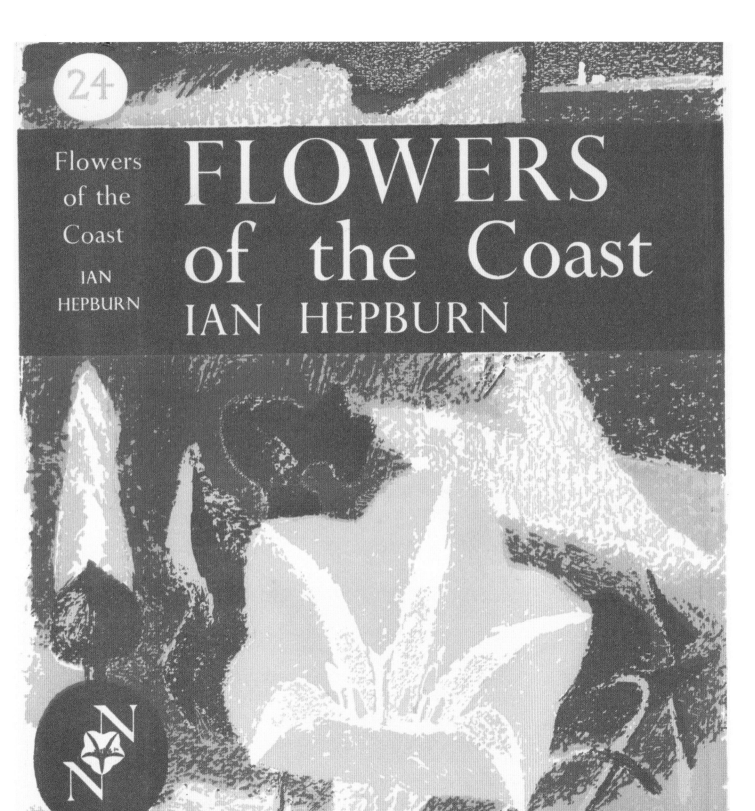

24

Flowers
of the
Coast

IAN
HEPBURN

FLOWERS
of the Coast
IAN HEPBURN

COLLINS

25 The Sea Coast

J. A. Steers, 1953

OPPOSITE The artwork of *The Sea Coast* substitutes red for the pinkish-brown colour on the printed jacket. It seems it was painted onto the jacket artwork by the printers, Odhams Ltd, to help guide the blockmaker. This was probably the 'mutilation' complained about by Clifford over the production of this jacket and that of the next volume, *The Weald.*

The author, Professor Steers had given some thought to the jacket of *The Sea Coast.* He suggested three ideas, or sets of ideas:

1. A close-up of a lighthouse with a rocky coastline in the background, 'symbolic of watching our coasts'
2. A tuft of marram grass or some other vegetation with sand dune or salt marsh in the background.
3. Some coastal phenomenon, such as an arched stack or strangely shaped rock in the foreground, 'likely to arouse the curiosity of the general public'.

What he decidedly did not want was any birds or animals (conveyed to CE by RT, 4.9.50).

C&RE took up the general thrust of these ideas, although their eventual design was closer to the author of *Flowers of the Coast,* Ian Hepburn's suggestion of 'some windswept trees and bushes, bent over by the prevailing winds, on the skyline' (conveyed to CE by RT, 11.10.49).

For the first version of the jacket, C&RE incorporated a lighthouse, which ran down the spine. Either they or the editors were not happy about this, and the design was re-jigged, moving the lighthouse to a distant promontory and paring down the detail to a rather bleak scene of bent bushes and cliffs circling a bay. The spine was now a bare beach brushed by the blotchy branches of the windblown bush. The design required just two tones of brown plus turquoise, relying on overlaps for the rest. Though a vision of nature at its starkest, it said 'sea coast' boldly and clearly enough, and the sea is often that blue-green shade. Closer inspection reveals tiny, characteristic touches: the little tree on the distant foreland, the bands of surf washing towards the viewer.

The Sea Coast

J. A. STEERS

COLLINS

The
S a Coast

J. A.
STEERS

26   The Weald

S. W. Wooldridge and Frederick Goldring, 1953

<small>OPPOSITE Once again the printers added red to the jacket artwork to help them with the process of separating colours. The red corresponds to the dull green and the blue of the printed jacket. The green and blue tones were much fresher and brighter than the printed jacket. Watercolour, gouache and wax on watercolour paper with printing instructions in pencil.</small>

The Weald is a dry book. The author was an academic geographer who stuck firmly to his brief, and the reader expecting to read about the woods, trees, flowers and birds in the rural heart of southeast England was in for a disappointment. Raleigh Trevelyan was hoping for a compensating bright, cheery jacket. If so, he was disappointed again. For *The Weald* C&RE produced a landscape in which hedgerows and fields echo one another into the distance in a curiously flat vertical plane that defies perspective. There are no bright colours and no foreground. If you look closely, somewhere within the maze of fields a herd of sweetly rendered Friesian cows is quietly grazing.

The surviving artwork of *The Weald* seems to be an earlier, brighter version of the design. Trevelyan did not like it, lamenting the lack of 'fresh air, light and spring-like' colours (RT to CE, 7.5.52). Perhaps, he suggested, the cows should be brought forward. C&RE made some alterations to the jacket, but once again the printer failed to do justice to their conception. Even so, as Trevelyan later admitted, the jacket 'certainly grows on one, and I am now very fond of it, after all the hard things I said in the past' (RT to CE, 13.3.53).

27 Dartmoor

L. A. Harvey and D. St Leger-Gordon, 1953

Dartmoor can be a gloomy place, and the jacket of *Dartmoor* is certainly austere and uncompromising. The foreground, with the iconic stone clapper bridge and rush of water over dark boulders, is lively enough, but above it rises a dark, threatening hill on which unfriendly spruce trees are daubed. The river winds up the spine towards the deep-green title band, but this is not a Dartmoor to attract the tourists.

That was precisely the objection to it. By 1953 the publishers were pinning a great deal on the New Naturalist jackets to encourage sales (while trying at the same time to print them as cheaply as possible). Dartmoor had seemed a promising title but the text turned out disappointingly dour and effortful; 'We had to get the author to rewrite a lot of the text to degloomify it,' remarked Raleigh Trevelyan. And now, as if the gloom were catching, the book was to have a dark, dour jacket. It looks all right in close-up, admitted Trevelyan, 'but the poster effect is lost at a distance' (RT to CE, 15.10.52).

'What would sell *Dartmoor*?' replied Clifford (who had made a special journey). 'Most visitors come by car and view it from car or motor coach. We did consider using a close-up of a windswept mane-blowing Dartmoor pony stallion's head' (CE to RT, 16.10.52) but felt it was 'untrue' to the book. He also moved the clapper bridge closer to match what Trevelyan called the 'hit-you-in-the-eye trade requirements'.

Odhams the blockmakers did little to brighten the clouds. The line draughtsman had been 'a bit clumsy' and, as Clifford complained, 'nobody on the printers' staff really able to see with an artist's eye' (CE to RT 16.10.52).

28 Sea-Birds

James Fisher and R. M. Lockley, 1954

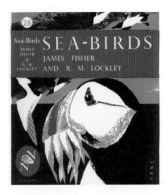

The jacket of *Sea-Birds* is dominated by a puffin. It was a doubly appropriate choice. In the previous year, one of the authors, Ronald Lockley, had written a book about puffins. And, apart from being delightful, puffins help to sell books. Allen Lane's Puffin picture books for children were at the height of their success at the time *Sea-Birds* was published.

For C&RE the main attraction of the puffin was probably its colourful bill and red eye, contrasting with its black-and-white body. It enabled them to revive their old trick of confining the brightest colour to the key element and focus of the design. The puffin's head and shoulders fill the panel beneath the title band. Three fellow auks (a guillemot and two razorbills) are flying in on the diagonal, while the underside of the wing of a third razorbill makes a fit subject for the spine.

The 'rough' of *Sea-Birds* was much admired, but James Fisher spotted something wrong. 'Entirely through my wrong briefing', he wrote, 'you have been asked to do a puffin holding fish in its beak with both heads and tails sticking out … The truth is puffins nearly always hold small fish in their beaks with only their bodies and tails sticking out … Thus the [fish's] head is normally invisible' (JF to CE, 31.5.50). The artists changed the design accordingly, but rejected Fisher's further suggestion of placing another puffin on the spine 'looking straight at you'. The National Book League chose *Sea-Birds* (and *Squirrels*) for its 100 Best Jackets for 1955.

Tim Bernhard, the wildlife illustrator and graphic designer, writes: 'When I first saw this jacket I was struck most by the apparent simplicity of the design, the bright cadmium-red of the title band and the main subject of a puffin's head. I love this quirky puffin with his slightly surprised expression, and bill stuffed with freshly caught sand eels. The background is a cool grey over which a flat indigo-blue is printed to represent the sea. The same tone is used for the textures of the fish and the puffin's face. The group of diving guillemots and razorbills introduces movement and life. And the design is completed with the bold use of black for the puffin's body and the head, tails and feet of the flying birds.'

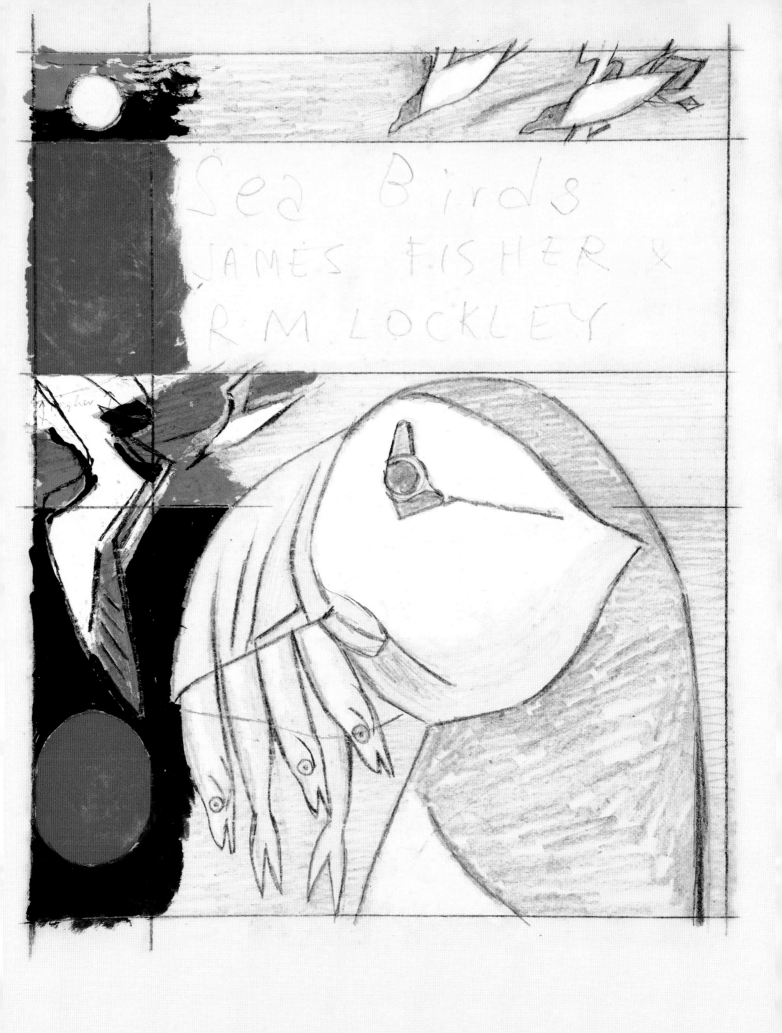

The World of the Honeybee

Colin G. Butler, 1954

OPPOSITE The artwork with printing instructions.

The World of the Honeybee was the first and, so far, only book in the mainstream series to be devoted to a single species. It was published in what Raleigh Trevelyan called a 'bastard size', smaller than other volumes in the main series but larger than the standard monograph size.

The book is full of monochrome images of bees and their honeycombs, swarming, feeding and raising their brood. A rival book on bees had recently been published, and Billy Collins wanted a contrasting style of jacket image, dominated by a very large bee. C&RE obliged, producing at very short notice a design showing a newly hatched adult bee emerging from its cell. The combination of the bee and the honeycomb, underlined by the rich orange honey-colour, linked the bee with the hive without calling for much colour or detail. This is a subtle design relying on overlaps for tone and texture, and the mesmeric quality of the repeated pattern. Its quality was partly lost on the reprints on which the orange ink threatens to overwhelm the design. Not knowing the width of the book, the black oval was drawn too wide.

Is this design a bit too simplified, and the Ellis bee lacking in sweetness? The message, perhaps, is that the hive is not a cozy place. However much we nurture them and enjoy the products of their labour, the world of the honeybee is nothing like our own.

orld
of the
Honey-
bee

COLIN G.
BUTLER

The World
of the Honeybee

COLIN G. BUTLER

COLLINS

30 Moths

E. B. Ford, 1954

TOP Sketch design for *Moths* at approximately half size, gouache and watercolour on typing paper with listed colours in pencil.

ABOVE The printed jacket.

OPPOSITE Artwork for *Moths* with printing instructions in pencil; includes gum marks where the work was fastened to the plate to be photographed.

Although it shared the same author, the jacket of *Moths* is nothing like *Butterflies.* Instead of a landscape with caterpillars, four fat-bodied moths are flying with unrealistic outstretched wings towards a narrow strip of brilliant light, perhaps a door left half open. It is night; the colours are dark and subdued. The attention is focused on the rich textures and patterns of the moths' wings: spots, zigzags, crescents and bands. They are an indication of the variety of moths that occur in almost any garden, hiding in the shadows as they await the dark.

The jacket artwork, printed opposite, has brighter, bluer colours than the printed jacket. There are also surviving sketches showing how the artists worked up a design from pencil and colour 'roughs'. The jacket is printed in three colours, purple-blue, blue-green and black. The title is outlined in huge mechanical capital letters on the black title band, made even blacker by overlaying with blue. The design was robust enough to sustain a succession of reprints without loss of detail.

The *Moths* jacket seemed to please everyone. 'Opening a parcel from Corsham,' exclaimed Raleigh Trevelyan, 'is almost as exciting as opening a Christmas present … wonderfully original and striking designs'.

Mark Parsons, a moth specialist working for the charity Butterfly Conservation, comments:

'The moths on this jacket are a mixture of fact and fantasy. The largest appears to be a Privet Hawk-moth, with its elegantly shaped forewings, while the one folding over the spine resembles an Oak Beauty. The spotted moth is a creature of the artists' imagination, though it is perhaps based on the pattern of a female Wood Leopard moth. The moths are presented in a rather impressionistic fashion and as they would appear in a collection, with their wings spread apart at right angles to their bodies. It is artistically pleasing, but rather dark and dingy, and of its time when there was more emphasis on collecting than there is today.'

Moths
E. B. FORD

MOTHS
E. B. FORD

N N
COLLINS

Man & the Land

L. Dudley Stamp, 1955

Man & the Land was a kind of sequel to Dudley Stamp's *Britain's Structure and Scenery*, describing the impact of 'man' as he settled and transformed the landscape. As usual, C&RE were sent 'pulls' from the book, including some of the plates, and left to wonder how to represent 'man' this time. William Collins put in his bit by suggesting a row of Lombardy poplars and 'better cows than sheep'.

Cows and poplars are fine in their way, but neither expresses the way we stamp ourselves on the landscape in ways that are clearly not all for the better. C&RE found a more unambiguous statement in the juxtaposition of a felled and a planted tree, the latter being on the spine inside its tree-guard. By a line of trees in the receding distance, black-and-grey cows graze obliviously in the middle distance.

Once again C&RE had come up with a neat and original summation of the book and expressed it with economy of colour (two greens and a grey). Yet the Board was less enthusiastic about *Man & the Land* than some recent jackets, feeling it looked a bit too much like *The Weald* and that the tree-stump image lacked the necessary impact. It did not help that, on the proof at any rate, Odhams had printed the colours in the wrong order and so the green 'lacks body'.

31

Man
& the
Land

L. DUDLEY
STAMP

Man & the Land

L. DUDLEY STAMP

COLLINS

32 Trees, Woods and Man

H. L. Edlin, 1956

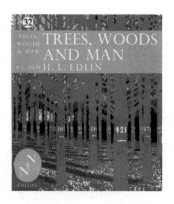

OPPOSITE Original design of
Trees, Woods and Man in gouache
and black chalk on watercolour
paper with printing instructions
in pencil. The oval symbol
and book number have been
'collaged' on.

Trees, Woods and Man was a favourite jacket both of the editors and the artists. It draws the eye into the dark ranks of trees, and the colours, black, brown and fresh green (printed in that sequence), harmonise beautifully.

The book came out at a time when traditional woodland management, such as coppicing, was becoming replaced by 'high forest' and plantations. In C&RE's vision, the trees are regimented in rows; they all look the same and the inference of the numbers painted on their trunks is that they are about to be cut down: trees in the service of man the planter and consumer.

As it happens, the numbers indicate otherwise. The author, Herbert Edlin, pointed out that the artists had in fact drawn a Forestry Commission 'sample plot' in which the trees are measured every few years to monitor their growth. Far from being 'doomed', they are 'saved'.

George Peterken, author of NN 105, *The Wye Valley*, and a distinguished woodland ecologist, comments: 'I chose *Trees, Woods and Man* when, for the only time, I was awarded a school prize, and I subsequently spent most of my working life working with the multifarious interactions between people, trees and woods. Quite why the Ellises' chose the interior of a maturing conifer plantation – the most industrial form of woodland management – is not explained. Perhaps they were attracted to the overwhelming regularity of the design and the opportunity to deploy a strikingly simple colour scheme of greens, relieved by black and white. The interlacing, rigidly geometric branches contrast with the parallel lines of the trunks and shadows, all free of interruption from untidy ground vegetation. The trees stand in lines, evenly spaced, all of the same size, and neatly numbered, so we are instantly aware of the depth of the perspective and the control exerted by the forester. The message is unmistakable: trees, aggregations of trees, and people are bound together. As an image it is arresting, and I was pleased, but not surprised, to see the original on display at a South Bank exhibition of landscape painting, 'Landscape in Britain 1850 – 1950' at the Hayward Gallery, London.'

32

369 421 370

C&RE

N° Trees, Woods and Man

3 colours, printed in the following order

33

Mountain Flowers

John Raven and Max Walters, 1956

I will never forget what Max Walters said about this jacket. We were talking about New Naturalists at his house in Grantchester by a window overlooking his wild flower garden. At some point he picked up *Mountain Flowers*, glowered at it for a moment, and said something like, 'What's this supposed to be, do you know?' He had asked the same question when he first saw the book. 'I would have preferred a recognisable plant on the cover,' he had grumbled, back in 1956.

No one knew the British flora better than Max, and he knew perfectly well that the delicate flower on the jacket of *Mountain Flowers* is the Twinflower, *Linnaea borealis*, necessarily in simplified form for a lithographic composition in three colours. Not choosing to recognise it was his way of saying he did not like the jacket. Neither, it seems, did the sales department at Collins. They thought the colours too cold and too similar to certain other New Naturalist jackets, notably *British Plant Life*. They felt the book needed 'a simpler design with more punch'. C&RE produced an alternative design but it was decided, on reflection, to proceed with the first one.

C&RE had seen enough of the text to know that the book was about the mountain setting almost as much as the flowers themselves: the climate, geography and the grand scenery of summits, corries and alpine lakes. The jacket captures the mood of an alpine scene on a rare cloudless day in the spring, the snowcapped hills reflected in the chilly, deep-blue water. The Twinflower, rooted off the page, was probably chosen for its delicate simplicity and the shape of its pendant, bell-like flowers.

It is impossible for me to judge this jacket objectively for it encloses a book I fell in love with. My first permanent job in nature conservation was in the Nature Conservancy Council in northeast Scotland, where I found myself the proud custodian of most of chapter six. There I found the Twinflower often, but never by the shores of a mountain lake. So what? Jackets are about selling books, not ecology.

Mountain Flowers

JOHN RAVEN
AND MAX WALTERS

33

Mountain
Flowers

JOHN
RAVEN
& MAX
WALTERS

COLLINS

C & R E

34 The Open Sea Part 1: The World of Plankton

Alister Hardy, 1956

Hearing that Collins was considering reprinting this venerable title in 1983, Clifford Ellis wrote to the new editor of the series, Crispin Fisher:

'*The World of Plankton* jackets have had a sad history. When this admirable book was first published in '56, the planktonic jacket we designed for it was scorned by the Sales Department as being too unfamiliar. So instead we provided a seascape. Quite recently a new jacket was needed so, assuming that in twenty-odd years the sales people might have become better educated, we did a new planktonic design. This seems to have pleased the author, nor did we hear of objections from the Sales Department. During the latter part of this twenty-odd years, however, there were not only changes in visual vocabulary but also in the costs of colour printing – and a beautiful jacket, ready for printing (not to speak of text and illustrations) were put aside. Hence our interest in what seemed to be a sign of life.'

The jacket was proofed but never printed, and the last and best of *The World of Plankton* jackets now hangs on the wall of the Collins reference books department above a cabinet with a complete run of New Naturalists.

The Open Sea was commissioned, as a single title, back in 1944. Alister Hardy belatedly produced an enormous tome which, by fortunate chance, could be divided into two books of roughly equal length, one on fish, the other on the small life on which all forms of marine life, from jellyfish to whales, ultimately depend – the plankton.

James Fisher thought it 'great fun that only plankton will do' for the jacket. The artwork for C&RE's first design survives, showing a planktonic 'medusa' in opaque gouache paint (the transparent inks used by the printer would have created a better impression of seawater). It caused some head scratching at Collins. 'Did you invent these animals,' Raleigh Trevelyan asked Clifford, 'or are they ones that exist?' (RT to CE, 31.8.54). They were, Clifford replied, 'faithfully rendered' from photographs and from direct observation at the aquarium during a recent visit to Naples.

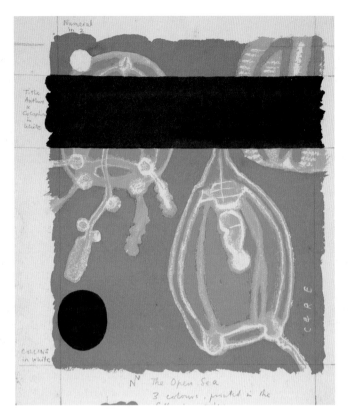

But it would not do. Trevelyan worried that the design did not convey any 'sense of mystery and movement in the open sea … There's something slightly static about [it], and it doesn't suggest vast oceans'. Most crucially, the 'the sales people' believed that the design would not appeal to book buyers since they would not understand what these strange creatures were. He suggested, instead, 'a design showing the sea, pure and simple, just waves' (RT to CE, 13.9.55).

So the artists prepared a second, wholly different jacket design expressing the 'mystery of the open sea'. In blue, green and black, it is a seascape seemingly lit by moonlight with a pathway of rippling reflections illuminating the green plankton floating near the surface. It is one of the more abstract designs of the series and one you could interpret in different ways. I used to see the top half as waves splashing against dark rocks rather than as a cloudy sky.

This jacket served throughout the lifetime of the book. The third, never published, jacket was another, more successful, attempt to show planktonic organisms. Alister Hardy was 'delighted with it … Whilst I liked the original jacket, I think this is so much more descriptive of the contents, as well as being most attractive. Clifford Ellis has caught the spirit of living plankton so well – I feel he must have drawn it from life.' Indeed, he probably had.

34

THE
OPEN SEA
The World
of Plankton

ALISTER
HARDY

THE OPEN SEA
The World of Plankton
ALISTER HARDY

N

COLLINS

CRE

The World of the Soil

35

Sir E. John Russell, 1957

The world of the soil is dark and wormy; animals living down there have poor eyesight but an acute sense of smell and an ability to tunnel and dig. Most of the beasties that appear in Sir John Russell's book are rather unprepossessing: grubs, millipedes, bacteria and worms of all kinds. As an agriculturalist he was chiefly interested in the soil's fertility and in the interactions of chemistry, weather and life that maintain it. But this is stuff for a diagram, not a jacket.

How do you sell soil? C&RE must have thought hard about it before enlisting the help of the soil's most charismatic inhabitant, the mole. But they were less interested in showing the whole mole, so to speak, than what the mole does. They concentrated on the animal's tunneling instrument: one of its spade-like fore-paws. Behind it is the dark mass of the animal's body in grey, its pig-like snout extending on to the spine (in later, darker printings of the jacket the mole's head is less easy to make out). The jacket design is rendered in strong, dark colours, brown, dark grey and black.

Trevelyan was 'very pleased indeed with your most striking jacket' (RT to CE, 4.12.56). The design is subtle and the mole obscure, yet the earthy tones, and squirls and speckles of colour, are intriguing and strangely satisfying.

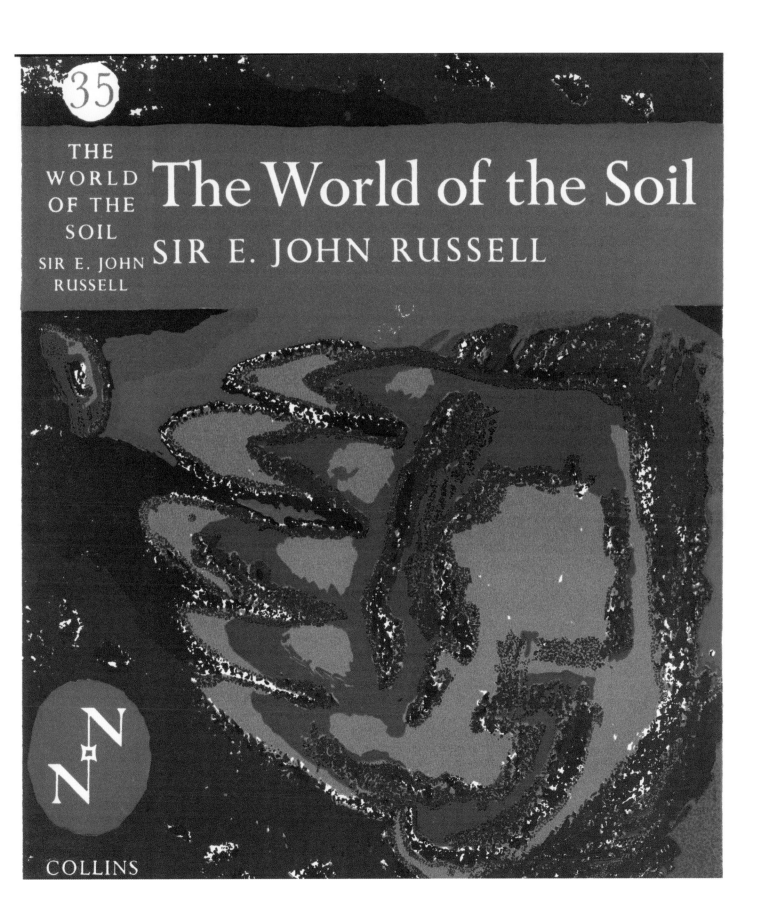

35

THE
WORLD
OF THE
SOIL
SIR E. JOHN
RUSSELL

The World of the Soil
SIR E. JOHN RUSSELL

COLLINS

36   Insect Migration

C. B. Williams, 1958

Searching for an image that conjures up the migrations of insects, C&RE considered including Clouded Yellow and Painted Lady butterflies before choosing the simple, bold, white-and-black outline of the Large White or cabbage white butterfly. The artists did some homework on the subject, discovering that migrating butterflies fly 'dead straight – even through railway tunnels!' We are in the midst of a mass migration, perhaps twenty feet above the ground and looking upwards into the butterfly 'snow storm'.

The design called for only three colours: pure blue, buff-yellow and black, letting in white as needed and printing yellow over blue for the shadows. The artists' use of black is sparing, and the overall effect is one of lightness and motion, a cloud of white wings on their way to England's cabbages.

The artwork, which was ready for printing by April 1957, was liked. That of the 1971 reprint of the book has a paler title band and oval, and a slightly deeper blue giving a sharper, more contrasted appearance.

Insect
Migration

Insect Migration

C. B.
WILLIAMS

C. B. WILLIAMS

COLLINS

37

The Open Sea Part II: Fish and Fisheries

Sir Alister Hardy, 1959

The second half of *The Open Sea* was published two years after the first in 1959 (the author had in the meantime been knighted for services to marine biology). In some ways *Fish and Fisheries* was a more straightforward jacket to design: compared with alien and commercially unacceptable plankton, one could envisage a commercially acceptable image of fish and fishing nets. While *The Open Sea* was still one book, its author, no mean artist himself, had suggested 'jellyfish or shoal fish' with 'fishing boats above'. The artists' first design was a 'wonderfully selling' one featuring some killer whales, but was rejected on the understandable grounds that the text fails to mention them! (RT to CE, 23.8.55)

C&RE thereupon came up with a design that matched Hardy's suggestion, but with their own take on life at sea. Back in the 1950s, many smaller fishing vessels were rough, rugged craft with masts, smokestacks and, often, sails. It was a hard life on cold rough seas, searching for the herring not by echo-sounders but by the movements of sea-birds and the tell-tale traces of fish-oil in the water. The artists' design showed their life as it often was: alone on vast waters on a windy, dark, overcast day, the breakers rolling, the sail rigged and the smoke streaming from the funnel. This is an inshore mackerel boat, hazy in outline, with a shoal of fish swimming just below the surface. The colours are sombre and in low tone: all greys and blue-greens, and both fish and fishers are shown in distant view to emphasise the immensity of the sea (reprints are printed on white instead of cream paper, and so appear slightly brighter). The boat's sail makes a neat emblem for the spine.

The jacket may lack some of its intended impact. At proof stage someone noted that 'something has gone wrong with the fish and the black doesn't look quite right on top of the blue sea.' (RT to CE, 5.12.57).

38   The World of Spiders

W. S. Bristowe, 1958

As if to prove that spiders, viewed sympathetically, are rather beautiful and amazingly diverse, the author Bill Bristowe privately commissioned the best entomological draughtsman of the day, Arthur Smith, to produce 230 drawings in line and wash for *The World of Spiders*. They help to make the book one of 'the best New Naturalists we have ever had', according to James Fisher.

From the outset, C&RE had decided that a web rather than an actual spider 'would be the right motif for the jacket – less difficult in colour and less fussy' (CE to RT, 9.9.57). Their orb-web does in fact show a garden spider, small and properly facing head-down at the centre of the web. It is outlined by a spot of rich reddish-brown matching the title band and oval. Against a richly textured background, the tight spirals of the web are caught in the light, and glisten with pure white accentuated by Ellis's favourite soft grey. The colours of the artwork are even richer than the printed jacket, and still show the faint pencil lines of the underdrawing.

Unfortunately this jacket is light-sensitive. It is rare indeed, nowadays, to find *Spiders* with its original rich red-brown colour on the spine.

38

CARE

3 colours in following order
① Black ② Red-Brown ③ Grey

N The World of Spiders

39 The Folklore of Birds

Edward A. Armstrong, 1958

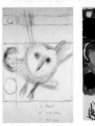

ABOVE Charcoal and colour sketches for *The Folklore of Birds* and the printed jacket.

OPPOSITE Artwork for *The Folklore of Birds* with number collaged on and printing instructions.

The Folklore of Birds was a title that William Collins tried hard not to publish. Commissioned in the heady days of the 1940s, when New Naturalists were selling well, the prospects for a scholarly book about an esoteric subject seemed less rosy ten years later. When the author held Collins to the agreement they had signed, the latter was minded first to cut colour printing to a single frontispiece, and then to deny the book an Ellis jacket, with the excuse that, as an 'art' subject, a jacket along the lines of *The Art of Botanical Illustration* would be more suitable.

In the end more generous councils prevailed, and for this Cinderella of a book C&RE produced one of their most striking designs, a barn owl swooping through the dark straight towards the reader. On the spine hangs a crescent moon close to the tail feathers of the owl. It is a mystical image, spooky but not frightening, appropriate to a book that is as much about superstition and psychology as about wild birds. The artists teased out a rich tone of dark blue for the night sky and the owl's deep eyes by printing opaque grey over black. Flashes of bright ochre outline the plumage, and the owl's mask is richly textured in grey on white. Since there is little pure black on the jacket, the artists could print the title band and oval in that colour without compromising the design. The composition is beautifully thought out and everyone, including the author and Billy Collins, loved it.

Of all the New Naturalist titles published up to 1985, this one had the shortest time in print. Book-lovers had less than four years to appreciate the Ellis owl.

Preliminary sketches for *The Folklore of Birds*, along with those of *The Rabbit*, were on display at the Crafts Council exhibition, 'The Decorative Beast', in 1990.

39

40 Bumblebees

John B. Free and Colin G. Butler, 1959

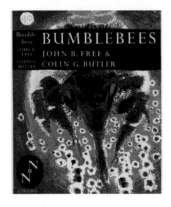

Like *The World of the Honeybee*, *Bumblebees* was originally listed as a 'special volume', but was eventually published in the 'bastard' format, size, larger than a monograph but slightly smaller than the rest of the main series.

The jacket shares the full-on bee-face of *Honeybee* but in other respects it is as different as the artists could make it. The *Bumblebees* jacket is richly coloured and full of vitality. C&RE's long-tongued bee is seeking nectar and pollen from a foxglove, and we see it head-on, as if from within the flower. This bee is probably modelled on the Common Carder-bee *Bombus pascuorum*, which is indeed fond of foxglove, though the latter was probably chosen for its lively internal pattern of spots and rich pinky-purple colour rather than strict biological conformity. The spots, together with the edge of the bee's middle leg, carry over onto the spine. Without careful inspection one would never guess that this colourful jacket uses only three inks (black, pink and yellow, printed in that order).

Billy Collins thought that *Bumblebees* and *Dragonflies* were 'two of the most lovely you have yet done'. If there is a problem, it is that most of the bumblebee's plump, banded body is hidden by the title band. This is an unfamiliar view of a bee and may not, as a result, shout 'Bumblebee!' loudly enough. It would make an equally good jacket for a book about pollination, and, nearly forty years later, and by coincidence (for he had not seen the rare *Bumblebees* wrapper), Robert Gillmor did indeed choose foxgloves and bumblebees in his design for NN 83: *The Natural History of Pollination*.

YELLOW

or

hon

TE

INS

te

N bumblebees

119

41 Dragonflies

Philip S. Corbet, Cynthia Longfield and N. W. Moore, 1960

Three years before *Dragonflies* was published, Clifford Ellis was sent a complete set of Sam Beaufoy's colour transparencies 'for inspirational purposes'. To help inspire them further, one of the authors, Philip Corbet, suggested the artists base their design on the Emperor dragonfly and its distinctive larva. The latter could squat on the spine, he suggested, while one or more newly emerged adults could inhabit the front of the book. There is more in the book about the Emperor dragonfly than any other species; Corbet had based his doctorate thesis on it.

Though the Emperor and its larva did make their way onto the jacket, they were barely recognisable. The artists were more interested in the way light plays on the wings of a dragonfly hawking along the edge of a lake than in precise details of its anatomy. Hence this dragonfly is seen in distant view, inside a lozenge of blue at the centre of the design framed by vertical banks and overhanging trees. The brilliance of the sunlight is increased by the dark tones (green overprinted by blue) in which it is enclosed.

This jacket, thought the editors, was 'one of the best the Ellises had produced'. William Collins wrote to congratulate them: 'I think it is amazing how you can go on year after year thinking out such lovely designs. The series makes such an effective display in the shops, largely owing to the designs.'

This is one of C&RE's more impressionistic jackets: the dragonfly hangs there for a moment, more reflected light than form or colour, and then is gone. We are left alone with the lake shimmering in the August sun and the dark trees rustling in the breeze.

DRAGONFLIES

Philip S. Corbet, Cynthia Longfield & N. W. Moore

COLLINS

42 Fossils

H. H. Swinnerton, 1960

OPPOSITE Artwork for the accepted jacket with printing instructions. The printed jacket failed to reproduce the full design on the spine.

BELOW LEFT Artwork for the rejected design of the *Fossils* jacket, gouache and chalk on watercolour paper with printing instructions in pencil.

BELOW RIGHT The printed jacket.

The original design for *Fossils* was a strange thing, a dark jacket showing the skull of a marine reptile, perhaps an ichthyosaur, preserved in the rock. C&RE might have sketched it from life (so to speak) from one of the dark-grey fossils from the 'Blue Lias' rocks of Lyme Regis. Its focus was the fossil's baleful eye socket, while its teeth would project around on to the spine on which the circle containing the series number stood out in white, like a full moon.

The Board did not like it, and this extraordinary design was rejected. The editors suggested an alternative in the form of an ammonite, whose tight spiral and segmented shell might make a satisfying pattern. The Ellises took up the idea and ran with it, creating a richly textured jacket printed in three colours, black, grey and orange. Two more fossils with radiating patterns, probably sea urchins, appear on the spine. The artists made more use of pure black than usual, and deployed it to lend form and depth to the ammonite. The colours are nicely balanced and give an air of immeasurable antiquity. With their usual attention to detail, C&RE had the title printed in huge capital letters to match the weight of the design.

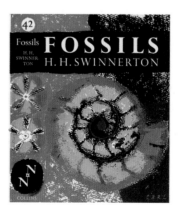

FOSSILS

Fossils
H. H. SWINNER-TON

H. H. SWINNERTON

COLLINS

C&RE

43 Weeds & Aliens

Sir Edward Salisbury, 1961

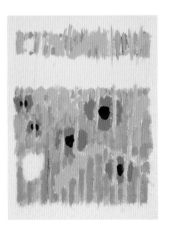

TOP The printed jacket.

ABOVE Sketch for the published jacket, full size, gouache and pencil on typing paper with notes in pencil.

OPPOSITE Sketch for alternative design of *Weeds & Aliens*, full size, in gouache paint on watercolour paper.

The bright and colourful jacket of *Weeds & Aliens* is a welcome ray of sunshine among the more sombre tones of its immediate neighbours on the shelf, and it has always been a favourite. The design is simple but strong: poppies, printed in the brightest of pure reds, peep through harvest-ready yellow cornstalks. Overlaps are minimal, though yellow on black provides some subtle variation in the stippled shade. The poppies are matched by a pure red title band. This sunny design was done in January. When the artwork reached the publishers, in April 1960, it 'was universally admired'.

Late poppies among the corn were an obvious choice for a book about 'weeds'. Yet the book's scientific editor, John Gilmour, had suggested, rather, a 'field with [blue] cornflowers' or else a design based on the flaring-trumpet shape and contrasting prickly fruit of a thornapple plant (this had received some recent notice in the press following a modest outbreak of poisonous thornapples in the Home Counties). A colour sketch of the 'thornapple alternative' survives: a dark jacket in cold violets and dark greens, contrasting with the flower's white petals. It might have made an interesting design, but with nothing like the emotive pulling power of bright poppies among the corn.

Weeds & Aliens needed a pretty jacket. Apart from a colour frontispiece the book is illustrated entirely in monochrome.

44 The Peak District

K. C. Edwards, 1962

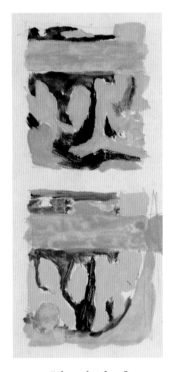

ABOVE Colour sketches for *The Peak District* jacket on cartridge paper, watercolour mixed with white and black (8.5 × 7.5 and 9 × 8 cm).

Perhaps the Ellises were happier designing jackets for titles about wild animals and plants than landscapes. Those they created for *The Weald* and *Dartmoor* were surprisingly bleak and rather forbidding, yet it was precisely these jackets that had most impressed the main author of *The Peak District*, Kenneth Edwards. He asked for something on similar lines, with the suggestion of a scene of 'moors and valleys', which certainly left plenty of room for interpretation.

For *The Peak District*, C&RE designed a claustrophobic landscape entirely in vertical planes, a narrow defile through the rocks, as if shattered by an earthquake, with a distant solitary tree beyond. Perhaps it was inspired by the sheer rocks of Water-cum-Jolly Dale shown in monochrome on Plate II of the book. All the rest is blocks and smudges in tones of green, the darkest of which is close to black. At one moment the jacket gives the impression of rocks with vegetation on the ledges and slopes below; at the next it seems to dissolve into an abstract composition, like one of Clifford's 'Untitled Lithographs' from the 1950s.

What the Board made of it is unrecorded. The minutes record only that it was 'approved with suggestions for improving the cleft in the rock'. The rate of production of New Naturalist titles had slowed down considerably by the time *The Peak District* was published, and this was the first new C&RE commission in more than a year.

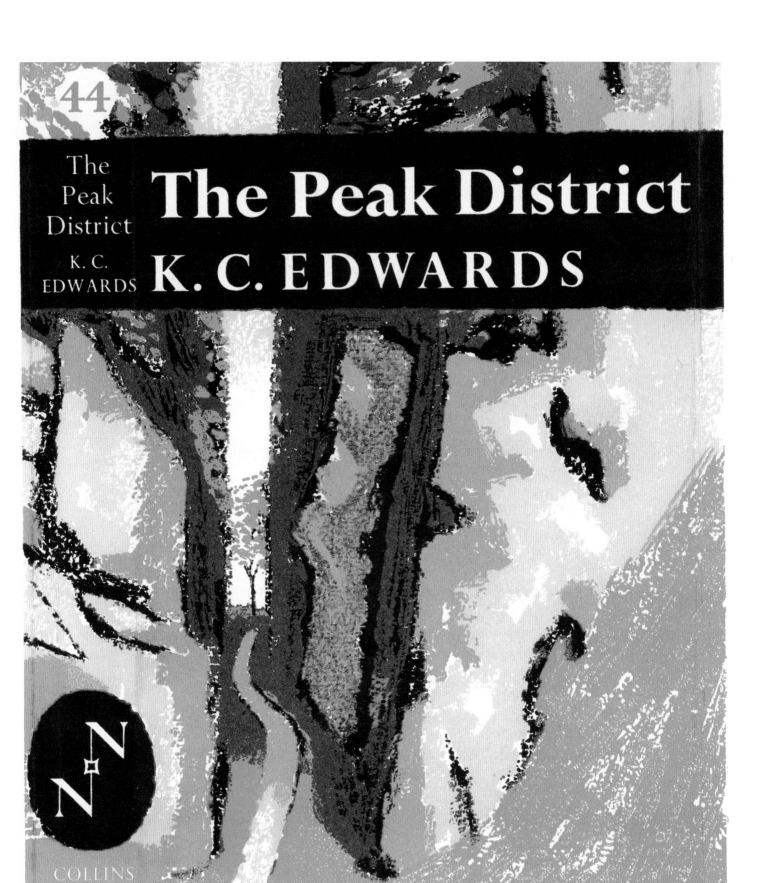

The Peak District

The Peak District

K. C. EDWARDS

COLLINS

The Common Lands of England & Wales

L. Dudley Stamp & W. G. Hoskins, 1963

This title was very much the creation of the Editorial Board, and was championed by its two most distinguished members, Sir Julian Huxley and Dudley Stamp (shortly to be knighted himself) over the reluctance of William Collins who, an editor recalled later, 'took against it for some reason'. Both Stamp and his fellow geographer, W. G. Hoskins, had been members of the recent Royal Commission on Common Land (which included village greens and urban commons), and Stamp was eager to bring its findings before a larger public. It was, in a sense, a one-off title, and there was some discussion about whether it should have a different, non-Ellis jacket; at one point Huxley suggested an old print of 'cricket or prize-fighting etc. on greens'.

Fortunately they changed their minds. This was the first new jacket C&RE had designed since *The Peak District*, more than a year ago, yet its colour tones, in greens and greys, are remarkably similar. The *Common Lands* jacket, however, is much softer, looser and easier on the eye. A donkey, with its bow legs and big ears, is grazing rough vegetation in the foreground while behind it a cricket match is in progress. The pure white of the cricketers (the batsman on the spine is leaning forward into his stroke), the umpire and the sightscreen form a vivid contrast with the tones of green. The donkey and the cricket match neatly capture the combination of use and pleasure which characterise our commons and greens; they also contrast athletic bowling and batting with quiet, placid chomping. It was as well the artists did not choose Morris-dancing as a theme; for the revised edition, Stamp had a plate (IIIb) replaced after a reviewer complained of 'too many Morris men'.

By some mischance, later printings of this jacket are taller by about a quarter of an inch than the binding.

45

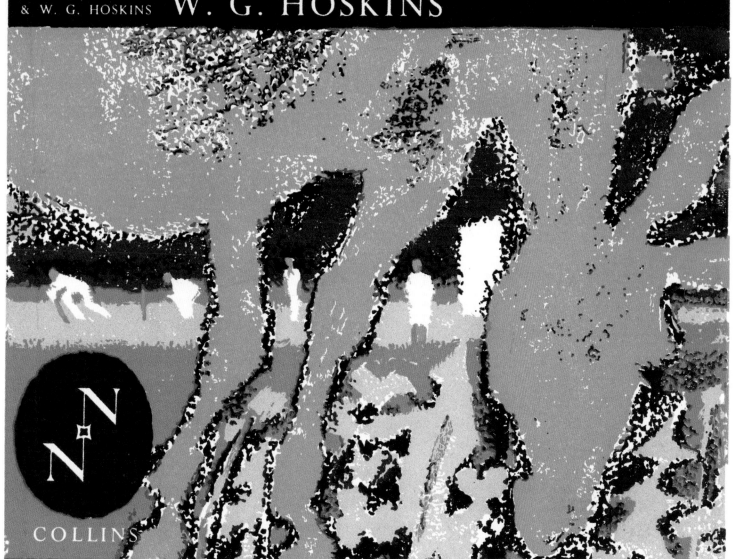

The
Common
Lands
of England
& Wales

L. DUDLEY STAMP
& W. G. HOSKINS

The Common Lands
of England & Wales

L. DUDLEY STAMP &
W. G. HOSKINS

COLLINS

46 The Broads

E. A. Ellis, 1965

One of the big selling points of the New Naturalist library, when it was conceived back in 1943, had been 'the latest methods of colour photography and reproduction'. Twenty years later, with falling sales, Collins felt that a nice colour photograph in tune with the changing times might be a better commercial draw than an artwork jacket. Perhaps, too, it was felt that landscapes had not been among the most successful of the Ellis designs. At any rate, for this long delayed 'regional' volume, the fateful decision was made to try out a new style of jacket. The Ellises were not brought into the decision. Shortly after publication, they received a letter from the Collins editor: 'You may have seen *The Broads* in the shops. It was decided to have photographic jackets for these volumes that have tourist appeal in a given region as opposed to the volumes for the serious naturalist' (Patsy Cohen to CE, 1.6.65).

Yet *The Broads*, as Ted Ellis and his helpers had written it, was not really a 'regional' guide book at all; apart from a chapter on 'Man in Broadland' and a brief discussion on river craft, it was pure natural history.

The irony was that *The Broads* had already received an Ellis design, not once but twice (and a third would follow before all was done). At a point when the book had seemed nearly ready, around 1955, C&RE had designed a jacket featuring the head of a great crested grebe with sailing boats in the background. The Board was unhappy with it since the grebe gave the impression this was a bird book (the bird content is, in fact, well throttled-back). Moreover, it resembled another colourful bird with a long beak, the woodpecker on the not-yet-published *Woodland Birds*. Nonetheless, James Fisher was eager to use it for a possible monograph on the great crested grebe.

In the meantime, the Board asked for a different kind of jacket with 'more light, clouds, with reeds and perhaps a sail in the distance. The central figure could be a windmill'. Billy Collins added a request 'to avoid getting the central figure overlapping onto the spine' (RT to CE, 13.4.55). When the text at last seemed nearly ready, in 1961, the Ellises were asked to produce such a design evoking the 'general feeling of the place' (Jean Whitcombe to CE, 28.7.61). Their design, which was probably never proofed, had a black band with sailing boats and windmills.

What *The Broads* eventually received instead of grebes or windmills was a vapid photograph of a sailing boat, a Norfolk wherry reproduced from a glass slide taken by John Markham (and the reproduction was poor, as one can see by comparing the jacket with the book's frontispiece of the same scene). The title was let in on a partial band near the bottom, but as a sop to disappointed collectors the spine retained the usual band, numeral and oval. Today the jacket looks dreary and forgettable, the laminated paper cracking with age. Some thought so even at the time.

By 1974, when a reprint was being considered, William Collins conceded that the new jacket had been a mistake; not only was it an aesthetic blemish but it had not, after all, succeeded in raising sales. The second Ellis design was dusted down and prepared by the new method of colour separations. It is an original and arresting image of a windmill reflected in water, using a lot of the artists' favourite turquoise. But it was never used. Ted Ellis never got around to revising the book, and so the bold new jacket by his namesake artists was not needed.

The jacket of this much-delayed book was eventually given a photographic jacket in the mistaken belief that it would have more popular appeal.

47 The Snowdonia National Park

W. M. Condry, 1966

The Snowdonia National Park was the first repeat title in the series (unless one counts *The Highlands and Islands*). Unlike the unwieldy and long out-of-print *Snowdonia*, Bill Condry's book was all of-a-piece and full of the sharp observation of a first-rate field naturalist. What it lacked, in the mid-1960s New Naturalist slump, was colour.

It also lacked an Ellis jacket. By coincidence, 'Snowdonia 2' came on the heels of another regional book, *The Broads*, and hence it fell foul of the new, and, as it turned out, strictly temporary, policy to dress regional books in photographic jackets. This time the jacket design incorporated a colour picture by Kenneth Scowen of a bog and some wooded hills, overlooked by the distinctive conical peak of Cnicht, 'the Welsh Matterhorn'. The jacket looked even less like a New Naturalist than *The Broads*. The editors, who claimed to 'like the idea of a photographic wrapper', might have had second thoughts when they saw it. At any rate, the experiment was not repeated, and the next title was back with an Ellis jacket.

THE
SNOWDONIA
NATIONAL
PARK
W.M.CONDRY

48   Grass and Grasslands

Ian Moore, 1966

Grass and Grasslands (the original title was to have been *Grass*, then *Grass and Man*) was conceived as a book about natural grasslands and wild species of grass. After the commissioned author, Cyril Hubbard, dropped out, an agriculturalist, Ian Moore, took on the title, and in his hands the book became more of a treatise on the use of grass for sown fields and lawns. In their preface the editors noted that 'the interrelationship between man and nature' had come to be an important theme of the series, though in this case nature seemed to be almost invisible.

Given that Moore's book is chiefly about replacing wild places with crops of grass, it is tempting to see C&RE's all-green jacket as a satire (though it was almost certainly not so intended). It is a view of a meadow as seen from a high vantage point through which a stream slowly winds. Along the banks are some 'lollipop' willows by which black-and-white dairy cows are safely grazing. But these are small details on a field that resembles a green baize card table.

The overwhelming 'green-ness' of the design was not intentional. The artists always specified the order in which the colours should be printed, but, it seems, in this case the printers (who had not handled a New Naturalist jacket for some years) made a mess of it. 'The spiky shadows below the trees bear no resemblance to the block pulls', notes an internal memo, and the printer had muddied the dark tones by printing them in the wrong order. In particular, the crucial black tone had been 'killed' by overprinting it with dark green. If properly followed, the design would have had far more punch. Even so, there is still something charming about the 'toy' cows and the reflections of the neat little trees in the cool stream.

Clifford Ellis often turned to the New Naturalist books for practical advice. He used this one to convince the college governors as to how the playing fields should be looked after.

49 Nature Conservation in Britain

Sir Dudley Stamp, 1969

Back in 1969, the public perception of nature reserves was as places set aside for wildlife. In the mind's eye, at least, they were surrounded by fences with a prominent sign reminding walkers to keep out. This gave C&RE the idea of a big traffic sign, a bright-red, circular 'No Entry' sign which, happily, made a marvellous contrast with dull green.

Nature Conservation was the editors' own contribution to the series. The main text had been written with his customary speed and efficiency by the now knighted Sir Dudley Stamp, but, after his untimely death in Mexico in August 1966, the typescript was left to his fellow editors, James Fisher and Kenneth Mellanby, to finish off. This took a long time, and it was not until 1969 that the book was ready for publication (though 'positively dripping with mistakes', according to an internal memo). The editors were by now in full agreement that the book should be graced by an Ellis jacket: no more photographs.

The germ for C&RE's bold idea might have come from Julian Huxley, who had a print of the ancient Abbotsbury Swannery in Dorset – arguably our oldest nature sanctuary – which at one point he was thinking of loaning for the jacket. The Ellises' scene is not Abbotsbury, though there are some distant swans on the lake behind the keep-out sign. It is probably nowhere in particular. Reeds form a nice pattern for the foreground, while the lake is fringed with trees with distant hills: it is a nice, quiet bit of countryside that deserves conserving.

The art editor, Patsy Cohen, considered this and the jacket of *Pesticides and Pollution* to be 'two most exciting designs' (PC to CE, 21.10.66). Unfortunately the *Nature Conservation* jacket was too complex to print by the usual method and a coarse screen had to be used for the overlaps – the hills and the grey-green reeds. That of the reprinted edition is in brighter, harder tones than the first edition. There is no record of C&RE's reaction, but elsewhere they mention that the poor reproduction of the jackets lay behind the decision to change the way the jacket artwork was prepared. The first title to benefit from the revision was *Man & Birds*.

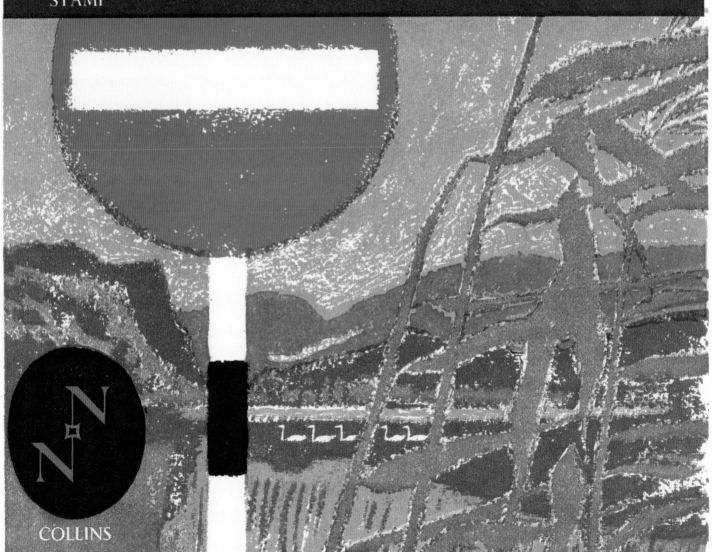

49

Nature Conservation in Britain

SIR DUDLEY STAMP

50   Pesticides and Pollution

Kenneth Mellanby, 1967

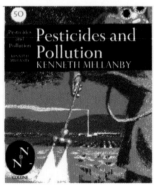

OPPOSITE This alternative design for *Pesticides and Pollution* was in brighter colours. The attached printing instructions suggest that it was sent to the printers but rejected, possibly because the latter were unable to reproduce it adequately. A new, darker version prepared by C&RE in three colours became the printed jacket (artwork and printed jacket shown above).

This, the darkest, most sinister of all the jackets, is an image of a world shrouded in smoke and poisonous fumes. Everything is wrong: the threatening sky is lavender and black, the crops are a horribly lurid turquoise, and the man with the knapsack sprayer is very sensibly sealed inside oilskins and a skull-like mask. The toxic chemicals enlisted in the service of man have come back to haunt us.

Pesticides were as much a public concern in the 1960s as global warming is today. Rachel Carson had been the first to warn of the insidious and frightening effects of poisons that did not decay but remained in the water or the soil, and were passed from plant to animal and so on in ever more concentrated form up the food chain to the top predators, like otters and peregrines, which suffered a lingering death. Kenneth Mellanby's book was by no means another *Silent Spring* but a more sober and objective, even apologist, account of pest control and its environmental impacts. But C&RE captured the fear that underlay the science.

This is a busy but nicely balanced design. The pure white, conical jets of pesticide (on a windy day like this he should not be spraying at all) establish a diagonal along the shaft of the sprayer completed by the man's partially visible helmet. Another plane is established by the horizontal plume of smoke which also adds an intriguing dimension to the spine. Yet another shape is formed by the curve of the hose. C&RE's habitual restraint is evident in the use of strong tones: the only pure black on the design (apart from the title band) is on the glass of the man's goggles.

There are two versions of this jacket whose artwork still survives. On the first, the sprayer's oilskins are bright yellow, the crops a more realistic shade of green and the sky a deep but environmentally friendly blue. It is not clear why a new and bleaker version was done; it might have been to reduce printing costs, or because the blockmaker could not make the first design work. For some reason the artwork for this version is half as large again as the printed jacket. It conveys a vision of environmental hell in black, turquoise and lavender that is among the strongest jackets of the series, though we doubt whether it is many people's favourite.

Nº Pollutions
& Pesticides
in Britain

3 colours printed in the following order
① Black
② Blue area (as bottom left)   DO NOT

51 Man & Birds

R. K. Murton, 1971

Man & Birds (and *The Mole*) was the first jacket to be produced by the new method of colour separations. It was published in 1971, just in time for a decimal price sticker, and the bold, bright jacket forms a sad contrast to the lack of colour within the book.

The Ellises had become dissatisfied by the reproduction of recent jackets. They proposed to switch to a demanding process in which each colour would be hand-drawn on white paper with the 'Pantone number' of the required ink added in pencil. This method enabled the jackets to be printed in-house at the Collins Glasgow printing factory (though it is possible that the blocks were still made elsewhere). Most of the jackets from 1971 onwards were printed in four colours, and so needed a sequence of separations to be combined by camera during the printing process. Clifford compared the process to reading the score of a quartet. Although C&RE always prepared a colour sketch of the design to help the printer, the full design did not appear until the jacket was proofed. The method requires skill and experience on the part of the artists, but the results justified the extra work. Many feel that the New Naturalist jackets of the 1970s are among the best in the series, with their bright colours and bold designs.

Characteristically, C&RE chose to symbolise 'man' by an artefact, in this case a church with a battlemented tower and flagstaff flying the flag of St George. The jacket uses four inks – red, black, blue and green – using overlaps to produce no fewer than three tones of black. The design also lets in a lot of white for the spire and the flag. 'Birds' are represented by rooks building their nests in the churchyard; one, with a twig in its beak, has flown uncomfortably close to us. Unusually, the title is picked out in red on black; the usual white lettering would in this case have detracted from the design.

This is a well-thought out design to inaugurate a new era. 'I think it's one of the most attractive there has ever been with this series,' said the new Collins editor, Michael Walter. Maybe, but that demonic, red-eyed rook is slightly disconcerting.

52 Woodland Birds

Eric Simms, 1971

Woodland Birds was on the first 'wish list' of New Naturalist titles made in 1943. Bruce Campbell had been chalked in as author, with John Markham, Eric Hosking and others providing specially commissioned photographs. Campbell did not find time to write the book. His successor as author, Brunsdon Yapp, did complete a book, but James Fisher found it too academic and stiffly written, and it was rejected (*Birds and Woods* by W. P. Yapp was published instead by Oxford University Press in 1962). It was only when Eric Simms accepted an invitation from Fisher to write the book that real progress was made. Simms' book was in fact ready by 1968 although it was not published until 1971.

c&re had designed a jacket for the Yapp book in 1955 (when it would have been around number 30 in the series) – 'a delightful painting' of a Great Spotted Woodpecker which sat in the bottom drawer at Collins for a decade and a half. When the time for its use finally arrived, c&re were asked to re-draw the design using the kind of colour separations that had proved so successful for *Man & Birds*. The new design differed in many small details, and the background was changed to an autumnal sepia and red in 'recognition of the exceptional autumn of 1970'. The woodpecker's distinctive red patch on the back of its head is carried over onto the spine – an idea the artists repeated on all their subsequent jackets featuring a bird. The same bright red was used for the title band and oval.

This jacket is to some extent a throwback to the early books in the series. The artists devoted close attention to the woodpecker's eye and beak, and, for the purposes of projecting onto the spine, its head is angled back as if, in a split second, it will drum its beak into the flyleaf. The background is only sketched in, and the turquoise trees are, to my eyes at least, sketchy and lack conviction.

52

Woodland
Birds

ERIC
SIMMS

Woodland
Birds
ERIC SIMMS

COLLINS

53 The Lake District

W. H. Pearsall and W. Pennington, 1973

The Lake District was another fated title that progressed at a snail's pace. It was among the projected National Park titles commissioned in the 1940s, in this case with the Carlisle-based naturalist Ernest Blezard as lead author and no fewer than five other contributors. The photographer J. A. Jenson had taken a set of 'breathtakingly good' glass slides for the book, but, unfortunately, the matching text proved less breathtaking, and was, in fact, never completed. Then W. H. Pearsall, the author of *Mountains & Moorlands*, took it up, but he never seemed to get very far with it either, and by the time of his death in 1964 had burned the draft in disgust, leaving only some notes behind. The book that finally emerged was basically Winifred Pennington's (Mrs T. G. Tutin), with some help from specialists, including four NN authors, Gordon Manley, T. T. Macan, Winifred Frost and Derek Ratcliffe.

In Pennington's hands, *The Lake District* was essentially a book about ecology and the physical landscape, though it was categorised as a 'regional' title. Had it been published in the late 1960s, as planned, it would probably have received a photographic wrapper. Fortunately it was now 1973 and the Board 'agreed to revert to the Ellises for the jacket'. Their only request was that the design might somehow incorporate the National Park symbol, a graphic representation of mountains and lakes.

The Lake District jacket is a demonstration of the virtues of more transparent inks, and makes an interesting contrast with the same kind of scenery on the much more dour *Mountain Flowers*. There are mountains and lakes, to be sure, but in the foreground and around the shores of the lake lies a host of golden daffodils, whose effect is nicely captured by letting in white within the brightest of yellows. The lake ripples in the dappled light, a cloud passes overhead and a cold breeze flutters the flowers. The jacket is inviting and, despite its simplicity, true to nature. Unusually, the oval is not picked out in a contrasting colour but in a tone. In the right foreground, in a patch of grass free of daffodils, the artists drew the letters 'WW'. This jacket was, after all, a homage to William Wordsworth.

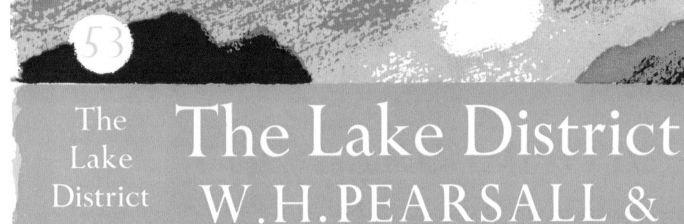

The Lake District
W. H. PEARSALL &
W. PENNINGTON

COLLINS

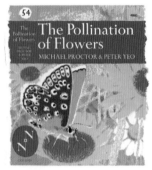

54   The Pollination of Flowers

Michael Proctor and Peter Yeo, 1973

For this jacket, C&RE produced one of their most luminous designs, a sunny close-up of a butterfly feeding on a daisy flower. Simply looking at it makes one feel happy. Unusually, the image is a magnification: the butterfly, a carefully rendered Adonis Blue, could in reality sit on a postage stamp.

It is a pity C&RE did not do more butterflies because this one is excellent: its black eye, flexible, zebra-striped antennae and powder-blue whiskers are well observed and lifelike, and the artists achieved a reasonably convincing brown by overlapping orange and blue. Most of the design is in three colours: blue, orange and yellow. The brightest, red, is reserved for the centres of the yellow daisies and the eye-catching spots on the butterfly's hind-wing. This leaves the artists free to blare it out on a title band which almost calls for sunglasses.

The Pollination of Flowers was a considerable academic achievement, 'a big, complex and valuable book' in John Gilmour's judgement. Had it been published twenty years earlier (or thirty years later), it would have been colourful inside as well as out. Michael Proctor, an expert plant photographer, had spent years patiently capturing the interactions of insects and flowers on colour film, often using state-of-the-art methods. But, because of the costs of colour printing, most of them were reproduced in monochrome (in Tokyo, as it happened). C&RE's jacket is a reminder of what might have been.

OPPOSITE Artists' colour separations for the jacket, each drawing prepared for a specific colour. These are reproduced at almost a quarter of their original size of 28.4 × 23.3 cm.

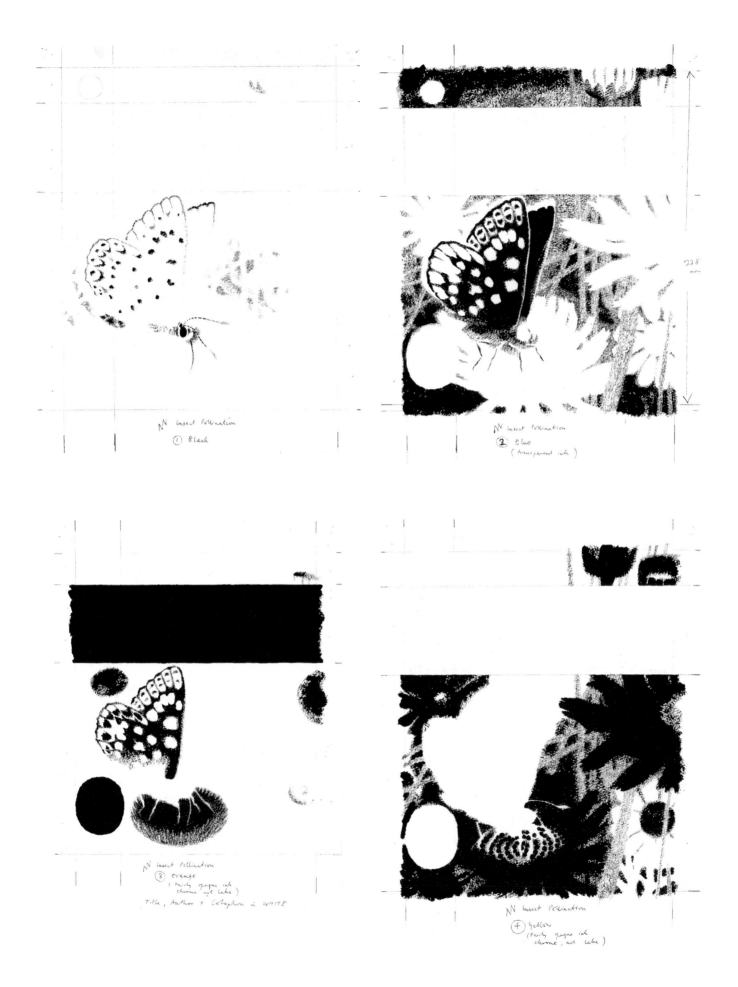

Insect Pollination
① Black

Insect Pollination
② Blue
(transparent ink)

Insect Pollination
③ Orange
(Fairly opaque ink
chrome, not lake)
Title, Author & Colophon in WHITE

Insect Pollination
④ Yellow
(Fairly opaque ink
chrome, not lake)

55 Finches

Ian Newton, 1972

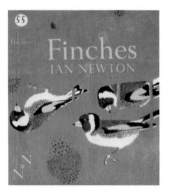

This title was published out of sequence, shortly after *Woodland Birds*. The young Ian Newton, who later became associated more with sparrowhawks and other birds of prey, was a professional research ornithologist. His book is often hailed as the best bird book in the series, a standard-setter and, in the words of one reviewer, 'a model of clear and logical writing'. Contracted to write the book at the end of 1968, Newton completed it in just over a year.

C&RE's colourful jacket, which was done at about the same time as *The Lake District*, was based on studies of goldfinches feeding on the teasels in the couple's front garden. The design intended the goldfinches to gleam brightly against a low-tone background of blues and greens, but, since the jacket was printed from colour separations, the blockmaker had no way of gauging the result until it was printed. He simply followed the artists' instructions. The 'pull' (or proof) of the jacket was disappointing, for the 'bilious' green was too dominant and 'oppressively egg-like' (Michael Walter to Ian Newton, 17.8.72). The printer overcame the problem by reversing out the original yellow from the title lettering, and substituting a gentler tone of yellow to produce a softer, more olive-green title band. The result was a much cleaner-looking and nicely balanced design, a snapshot of life with the finches, full of movement and colour.

Everyone loved it. On 3 January 1972, Billy Collins wrote to say how much he admired the most recent designs: 'I was looking with Patsy [Cohen] last week at your designs for *The Lake District* and *Finches*. I think they are two of the loveliest yet that you have done, and with *Pollination* and *Woodland Birds* they will make a tremendous display. I do think your wrappers are better than ever. We owe so much to you and I think it is marvellous after all these years that you should be keeping up such a terrific standard' (WC to CE, 3.1.72). This stamp of approval for the separations process must have been a great encouragement to Clifford and Rosemary at the point when they were about to retire from teaching.

55

Finches

IAN
NEWTON

Finches
IAN NEWTON

COLLINS

149

56

Pedigree: Words from Nature

Stephen Potter and Laurens Sargent, 1973

In June 1972, Michael Walter warned Clifford that an unusual New Naturalist title was coming up, one which dealt not with wildlife or natural habitats but with words. 'It will be fascinating to see what you eventually choose to feature in the jacket,' he said.

C&RE's solution was a kind of word puzzle. The jacket includes the Greek and Latin forms of the word 'Geranion', among a collage of flowers, seed-heads and the head and bill of a crane. Readers of the book will soon find out what it is all about in chapter one. But here, in a note Clifford made at the time, is the meaning behind the artwork:

> 'Geranion – GERANIUM – Cranesbill
> Modern botany began with a concern for old words.

> 'The great renaissance herbalists did not presume to give new names to plants. As men of their time, they accepted unquestioningly the authority of the newly accessible classical authors. As herbalists, however, they had the special challenge of identifying the plants which their authorities had named. This identification is what William Turner wrote about in 1548 in his book, called, significantly, *Names of Herbs*.

> 'One kind of plant has a long-beaked fruit "lyke Cranes heades"; the Greek name was *geranion*, from Geranos, a crane. The Latin form of that name was *geranium* and Turner identified "a kynde, called in English Pinke nedle or Storkis byll". Of these English names, the first is not a bad one for, say, Herb Robert, "byll" whether, storkes or cranes, more closely confirmed the identification with *geranium*, and was therefore what was wanted in the sixteenth century. Since then the Latin name of this plant has continued to be *Geranium robertianum*.

> 'The plant shown on the jacket is Meadow Cranesbill, *Geranium pratense*. This

name has remained unchanged by botanists since its incorporation by Linnaeus into his systematic naming of plants, published in 1735. The bird's beak is that of the Common Crane, whose scientific name is not Geranos in Greek but Grus in Latin.

'Latin names are not necessarily scientific names, and geranium has interestingly different uses. From early in the seventeenth century, some newly discovered plants were increasingly brought to Europe from South Africa. These too were called *geranium*, although from the end of the century the common name for the African plants tended to be Storksbill, to distinguish them from the European Cranesbill...

'The division which is still followed today by botanists, was made in 1787 by Charles Louis L'Heritier de Brutelle ... L'Heritier named a new Order, Geraniaceae and divided this into three, keeping the name *geranium* for his first and typical genus (the native European cranebills), and calling the others after more birds with long beaks for which there were Greek names: *pelargonium* (pelargos, a stork) for the African genus and *erodium* (erodios, a heron) for the third genus, which disconcertingly has the popular name of Storksbill ... His names, however, were arbitrary code words: the form of a stork's bill did not especially resemble the fruit of a Pelargonium more than it did that of a Geranium or Erodium. This may partially explain why the new names did not affect popular usage.

'Among the plants from South Africa there were some with flowers of a sensationally brilliant scarlet. Europeans soon found they could grow them in their new glass houses or in the windows of their homes and, when there was labour, bed them out in the summer. The many cultivated forms of these plants (which were some of L'Heritier's *pelargonium*) are, nearly 200 years later, still known to most people by their Latin but now unscientific name of *geranium*' (CE 13.9.72).

British Seals

H. R. Hewer, 1974

Humphrey Hewer, the author of *British Seals*, probably never saw this beautiful jacket; he died suddenly in 1974, a few days after correcting the proofs of his book. Originally commissioned as a 'special volume', the book made it into the main series after the effective demise of the monographs.

The jacket is one of c&re's undoubted masterpieces, giving a vivid sense of how a seal moves through the water, almost effortlessly. The blue and green inks, chosen for their transparency, create an aqueous effect that would have been impossible with the earlier generation of printing inks. The jacket needed only one minor amendment: the triangular highlight in the seal's eye was made a little smaller. *Seals* was published at a time when each new Ellis jacket was often praised as the best ever. 'The seals jacket is (in my view) the best you have ever done', wrote Michael Walter. 'It really is wonderful' (mw to ce, 24.1.73).

Clifford explained the background to the jacket in a letter to Michael Walter:

'The seals are a consequence of a visit to the London Zoo where I could be sure of seeing a pike in the aquarium to stimulate further thoughts about *Patterns in Nature* [a book that Collins was hoping to publish]. From time to time I went out into the bitter wind to watch the seals and how they swim – like monstrous trout, an extraordinary adaptation. I don't know whether the text is now complete, but the author may like a present of the French *accouder*, which says for the fore limbs what to kneel says for the hind ones. He will know better than I that the seal doesn't use only the flipper but, with great versatility, the whole limb, and when ashore … may support itself on its elbows like an old lady at her window-sill. Habitual, but, in English, nameless.'

A few technical details: the jacket was printed in four colours (black, ultramarine blue, cold slaty grey and pale blue-green, in that order) on 'Snoscene' and durasealed. The pages were printed by letterpress 'on Esparto Antique Wove and sewn cased in standard green buckram on 1750 micron strawboards, blocked on the spine in Newvap.'

57

57

British
Seals

H. R.
HEWER

British Seals

H.R.HEWER

COLLINS

58 Hedges

E. Pollard, M. D. Hooper and N. W. Moore, 1974

OPPOSITE Pencil studies for the *Hedges* jacket, on cartridge paper, folded over to make two sheets, each 12.7 × 20.2 cm. They were used for the right top of the jacket design (above), above the title band.

This title came about after James Fisher had heard a 'brilliant' talk by Max Hooper about how hedges could be dated by counting their constituent species of bushes and trees (a method now known as 'Hooper's Law'). Hooper was a scientist with the Nature Conservancy at Monks Wood Experimental Station in what was then Huntingdonshire. With his colleagues Norman Moore and Ernie Pollard ('Mellanby's Monks-wood minions', as Fisher had laughingly referred to them), Hooper had made a detailed study of the importance of hedges for wildlife as well as their steep rate of decline; for at that time, progressive farmers were busy turning Huntingdonshire from a county of small fields and hedges into a prairie.

In the way of multi-author books, *Hedges* took several years to finish, but it proved a success and was reprinted three times. 'After a few years in which the New Naturalists have seemed to tend towards the pedantic and the overspecialized', wrote Jon Tinker in *New Scientist*, 'the book is a welcome return to the series' earlier aims of scientific knowledge set firmly in the context of nature.'

The jacket design, a May-time roadside in spring-fresh colours, turns on the two little dabs of pure bright colour on the Orange-tip butterfly contrasted with the greenery around it. Clifford's instructions to the printer were to render the orange as brilliantly as possible. He was overheard repeating this over the telephone: 'Remember the colour must be brilliant,' said Clifford Ellis. 'Brilliant.'

So it was, and so is the jacket. The composition uses fresh-green, dark green, pale blue-grey and orange, the latter otherwise used only for overlaps to obtain brown. The trick of carrying some of the fresh-green into the title band and oval works well. The butterfly flutters along a bank of frothy cow parsley and lady's smock by a winding lane. In the distance are trees, hedges and the bare earth of newly planted fields. It is a May morning somewhere in England, and the landscape, though wholly man-made, is sweet and serene.

Unfortunately the jacket was sealed inside cheap plastic wrappers so we see this lovely scene as if through a dirty windowpane.

155

59 Ants

M. V. Brian, 1977

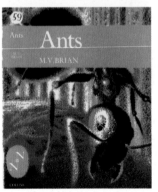

ABOVE Alternative jacket design with two ants. Full size, gouache on watercolour paper.

OPPOSITE Another version of the *Ants* jacket tries the effect of the title band in red. Gouache and pencil on watercolour paper with pencilled notes.

'We must get a good book on ants,' said Sir Julian Huxley in 1961. The monograph, *Ants* (1953), by Derek Wragge Morley, was, for various reasons, not considered a good book. An eventual replacement author was found in Dr M. V. Brian, one of a band of Nature Conservancy scientists who made such an impression on the series in the late 1960s and '70s. Brian certainly knew his ants, but he was not blessed with the common touch. 'He's trying to make his writing a bit more appetising', noted Kenneth Mellanby in 1972. Perhaps in consequence, the book was long delayed. C&RE designed the jacket in 1973 but the book was not published until 1977.

The jacket shows a wood-ant in monstrous close-up within a forest of grass-blades, looming towards the viewer with open jaws, ready to squirt us with formic acid. In what was to be his last letter to the Ellises, Billy Collins told them he thought this jacket was 'the best you have ever done. It knocks the first *Ants* into a cocked hat' (WC to CE, 26.3.74). It is not clear whether Collins was referring to the jacket of the monograph title, *Ants*, or to an earlier version of this jacket which shows a pair of ants. If the latter, some might disagree. While the ant on the printed jacket is undoubtedly more dynamic, the rejected version has its merits, notably in the carry-over of the ant's red-glinting body onto the spine (that of the printed jacket has to make do with a trailing hind-leg).

All lettering
WHITE

Numeral
DARK ORANGE

N° Ants

REVISED, with green
band & colophon & more
b. sienna

60 British Birds of Prey

Leslie Brown, 1976

OPPOSITE Sketch of the design of the *British Birds of Prey* jacket, full size in gouache and pencil on thin cartridge paper.

A New Naturalist on birds of prey was always likely to be a popular title, and Leslie Brown's book sold more than twenty thousand copies over ten years. The expatriate Brown lived in Kenya and made two extended trips to Britain in which he watched all the resident birds of prey, and caught up on the latest research (and that was a lot). He cheerfully predicted that he would be accused of 'poaching', and he was. Begun in 1969 and completed in 1972, the book was not published until 1976. Brown blamed the publishers; the publishers blamed Brown for being so far away and so seldom at home (at one point he was locked up in jail after a misunderstanding with the Somali authorities). The file on *British Birds of Prey* makes entertaining reading.

C&RE designed the jacket in 1971, and it received the by now customary applause from the publishers. Billy Collins thought it 'quite beautiful, the best yet'. 'I think it is one of the nicest in the series,' agreed Michael Walter (MW to CE, 12.3.76). 'It is a vindication of the printing method we evolved,' replied Clifford. The softly drawn design is of an adult male sparrowhawk in full flight. The colours of the bird allow the background to be rendered in rich tones of reddish-brown and ochre (the base colours are orange, grey, ochre and black, the latter used only for overlaps). The hawk's flight feathers extend the design above the title band while its long, barred tail carries over onto the spine. The latter is perhaps the weakest point of the design: the tail does not shout 'bird of prey' in the way that a beak or talon might have done.

From a collector's point of view, a greater problem is that the red-brown ink chosen for the title band is light-sensitive. Moreover, the publishers seem to have economised by reprinting the jacket on thinner, inferior paper on which some of the rich-toned effect of the original has been lost.

6 1   Inheritance and Natural History

R. J. Berry, 1977

How to give pictorial expression to so abstract a subject as inheritance? C&RE had two ideas. One was a pair of Peppered Moths, one in typical pale colours, the other the dark melanic form which predominated in industrial areas. The other was a 'mouse in a remote place connected with past human activities'.

Mice are believed to have been introduced to the northern isles by the Vikings, and over time they have developed characteristics distinct from those of their ancestors on the mainland. The Ellises chose one of these ancestral mice for the jacket, showing it looking down on the huts and beached ships' hulls on the shore with more Viking ships sailing above the title band. Near the mouse is a tuft of Sea Campions, another species well-studied by geneticists and one which had already been seen on a jacket (*British Plant Life*). The tones are cool – all greys and blue-greens except for the warm orange mouse dominating the design. As usual, the artists are sparing with black, reserving it for tiny patches of shadow.

Inheritance is a challenging book, possibly the toughest in the whole series. It makes genetic research as accessible as possible, but the publisher's reader confessed she had hardly understood a word of it: 'he's done a convincing job but the subject seems to be occult'. Moreover, none of Berry's subjects – rats, mice, snails, spittle-bugs – 'have appeal except for their genes'. Anticipating poor sales, Collins printed this book on the cheap. The handsome black letterpress hitherto associated with the New Naturalist library was replaced by grey, eye-squinting, micro-printed filmset on thin paper.

The jacket, fortunately, escaped the penny-pinching measures. Clifford 'is very fussy about [colour] matching, and knows a great deal about it,' Michael Walter warned the printers. A proof came with the rather lame comment that, 'we think it looks very nice'. Clifford replied: 'It is nearly right. The grey, though the right tone, would have a more lively effect in the colour scheme if it matched the specified Pantone 549, i.e. if it had slightly more "Reflex Blue" and slightly less "Yellow". I am glad you like it. P.S. Perhaps "COLLINS" should be a little larger and bolder.'

Inheritance
and
Natural
History

R. J. BERRY

Inheritance and Natural History

R. J. BERRY

COLLINS

62 British Tits

Christopher Perrins, 1979

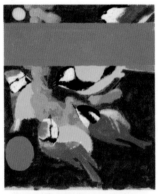

ABOVE A much darker sketch design of *British Tits*, full size, gouache on tracing paper with notes in pencil.

BELOW Detail from a sheet of pencil studies of Blue Tits and Great Tits made by Clifford Ellis in February 1940 (whole sheet 44.5 × 54.5 cm).

Shortly before *British Tits* was published, the author, Chris Perrins, received a proof of the dust jacket in 'a rather lurid yellow'. He did not much like it, and neither did the editors. 'At least two of the reject jackets remained in the Collins office,' recalled Perrins, 'but when I tried to retrieve them they were no longer to be found ... Are they still there, somewhere?' Though the answer to that seems to be no, the rejected 'yellow jacket' seems to have been a printing error. By some mix-up over instructions, the design had been printed with glossy inks, and not matt as required. Clifford was 'bewildered' when he saw the proofs.

The printing of this jacket seems to have been troublesome, mainly because the background green is formed by overlapping blue and yellow. The design shows four species of tit feeding on a string of peanuts, based in part on pencil sketches the Ellises made by watching birds feed in their garden. When sent the proof, Clifford noted that 'The blue is wrong. In combination with the yellow (which is right) it makes a green that is too dominating' (CE to Libby Hoseason, 2.2.78). The solution was to substitute a deeper blue and a less gingery shade of buff. Though C&RE were not happy with the second proof either, the publishers refused to provide a third on the grounds of expense. Some may feel that the green is still too strong for the design to work really well.

Nevertheless, the jacket captures the distinctive 'jizz' of the birds: the acrobatics of the Blue Tits (one, whose head is slightly too big, has side-stepped onto the spine), the bold, slightly aggressive posture of the Great Tit, and the hesitant, almost apologetic presence of the Coal Tit, all faithfully rendered in blues, blacks and yellows, with a complicated overlap of orange, green and black for the duller feathers. Like real birds, it cheers us up.

British Tits

CHRISTOPHER PERRINS

COLLINS

63 British Thrushes

Eric Simms, 1978

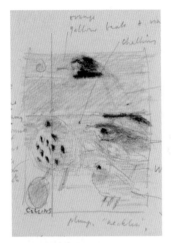

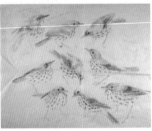

ABOVE Sketch for jacket design of *British Thrushes* with notes, pencil, coloured and black chalk on bond paper (20.3 × 12.7 cm).

Pencil sketch of 'Song Thrushes' (they look more like Fieldfares) by Clifford Ellis, February 1940 (whole sheet 44.5 × 54.5 cm).

At a warm moment during that longest and hottest of summers in 1976, Clifford Ellis decided to 'cool myself by thinking about NN *Thrushes* and snow' (CE to MW, 9.7.76). Though numbered after *British Tits*, this book was completed ahead of schedule and published the year before. The book continued the dominance of birds among the New Naturalist titles in the 1970s and '80s (8 out of 20 published between 1971 and 1985).

The chilly design of *British Thrushes* has a Blackbird, a Redwing, a Song Thrush and a Robin huddled together in the snow as though waiting for the crumbs to arrive on the bird table. The snowy backdrop allows the black and red colours to stand out strongly, while the pale parts of the birds merge into the snow. The blue-grey shadows are effective, and, characteristically, the strongest colour, yellow, is used sparingly, most notably for the blackbird's beak and eye.

There was only one thing wrong with the jacket and it was the Robin, the nearest bird to the viewer. *British Thrushes* had deliberately confined the 'small chat-like thrushes', including the Robin, to a final chapter, and, rather belatedly, the publishers felt it needed a jacket in which the Robin did not appear. 'That contentious robin' obliged the artists to produce an alternative design featuring a large and dominating thrush projecting above the title band with more birds on the snowy path behind. Yet the design seemed less lively, and in the end the editor decided that the inclusion of the Robin did not really matter.

This was a bright and cheery design that could easily have doubled as a Christmas card. It is a shame the colours are light-sensitive, for faded spines lose the subtle flickers of colour and soon look washed out.

British Thrushes has one more claim on our attention: the text is illustrated by Robert Gillmor, the future New Naturalist jacket designer (he also helped illustrate *Finches*).

164

63

British Thrushes

ERIC SIMMS

British
Thrushes

ERIC
SIMMS

N·N

COLLINS

64   The Natural History of Shetland

R. J. Berry and J. L. Johnston, 1980

The Natural History of Shetland came about from an offer by R. J. Berry, author of *Inheritance*, to orchestrate contributions to a multi-author book about the Shetland Isles, with the help of Laughton Johnston, a former schoolmaster, poet and local naturalist. Collins turned the idea down, then changed its mind after optimistic predictions of local sales, plus some largess offered by BP on the condition that the book would be a New Naturalist.

Clifford Ellis had never been to Shetland, and for this jacket he took a BP-sponsored flight to Lerwick in 1979. In gaps between the rain he sketched clouds and landscapes. His resulting design also took in Shetland ponies, an oil rig, fishermen's cottages and tugs butting into the tide along one of Shetland's narrow 'roes'. Fittingly for a time when the traditional life of Shetland was being transformed by North Sea oil, the jacket juxtaposes the old with the new.

The subject matter required a lot of blue, to which the artists added a warm grey that teased out extra colours when combined with blue and fresh green. C&RE were, as usual, economical with black, reserving it for a piebald pony, its mane blowing in the wind, and the hulls of the distant tugs. The sea shimmers, and the reflections merge imperceptibly with the hazy clouds of a Shetland morning. Yet the design hangs together less successfully than most Ellis designs, and the fuzzy grey head of a second pony is a serious weakness. It is probably there in an attempt to balance the detail on the spine, but looks like an afterthought. The earlier sketch reproduced here has the better balance.

Like other titles published in the first half of the 1980s, *The Natural History of Shetland* jacket was imprisoned inside a cheap plastic wrapper that did it no favours. The book was reprinted in 1986 on laminated paper, which gave a harder, brighter image but lacks the tonal quality that depends on a matt surface.

Numeral
green (583)

167

65 Waders

W. G. Hale, 1980

Of all the long-legged shorebirds, there could never have been much doubt about which one would star on this jacket. The oystercatcher is the perfect subject for a jacket design, its pure black-and-white plumage contrasting with that big red powerful bill. The bird in effect chose the colour scheme, and the artists' job was to make a pleasing, eye-catching composition from it.

What C&RE did, after some experimentation, was to arrange five oystercatchers in such a way that only one bird is in full view. The other birds are partly outside the picture, and one is visible only by its bill. The effect is like a snapshot, or a detail taken from a larger composition, and emphasises that most waders are social birds. It is winter, so the birds wear white collars; Clifford referred to the design as a 'Winter Synod of Anglican Oyster catchers'. The birds are softly drawn to increase the impact of that hard, dagger-blade of a beak coloured in the richest red the artists could find. Unusually, there are few overlaps; red, blue, pink and black are used mostly in pure form apart from some dark reflections on the water. The spine, in which the bird's head prods downwards as if to spear the oval like a cockle, is particularly effective. The result was, in the editor's words, 'rather striking'.

Charlotte Ellis remembered that this jacket was designed after a family trip to the Camargue in France.

Waders

Waders

W.G. HALE

W. G. HALE

COLLINS

66 The Natural History of Wales

W. M. Condry, 1981

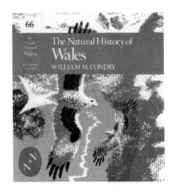

OPPOSITE Rejected alternative jacket design for *The Natural History of Wales* with a dipper perched by a waterfall. Full size, gouache on tracing paper.

William Condry wrote this book swiftly, and perhaps effortlessly, drawing on half a lifetime's experience of roaming the Welsh hills and coast. In the view of his assigned editor, Margaret Davies, 'Bill Condry has done [the book] as I hoped he would. It is so readable and thoughtful, and will make a very good volume in the series. I like his evocation of habitats, and readers will appreciate so much personal observation.'

The first jacket design, for which only a colour sketch survives, shows a dipper perched on a rock by a waterfall against a dramatic mountain background. It might have led to an outstanding jacket (with the waterfall running down the spine), but for some reason it was rejected. Instead, the artists decided to create a bird's-eye view of a pair of red kites circling over a Welsh valley, their forked tails splayed. Again, the basic idea is good: the birds and the U-shaped valley say 'Wales' as clearly as anything could, but the design as it appears on the printed jacket seems sketchy, as if it had been done in a hurry and left only half finished.

The colours, fresh green, blue-grey and reddish-brown, harmonise well. The design allows the tail of the lead kite to overlap on to the spine, but instead of the expected rich red tone we find only the pale under-feathers. The birds are freely drawn to the point of crudity, especially the primary wing-feathers. And, with so many recent bird titles, one might question the choice of yet another bird as the main subject.

Exceptionally, first edition copies have the figure '66' stamped on the buckram spine of the book.

Farming and Wildlife

Kenneth Mellanby, 1981

Like *Waders*, this jacket used a lot of pink. This time the colour (in a slightly colder tone than on *Waders*) is used to create a vivid sunset (or sunrise?) against which the lapwings swoop past on their broad, crooked-back wings. The jacket uses a remarkable combination of colours – pink, blue, green and brown – though the design fails to connect wildlife and farming quite as clearly as, say, the jacket of *Birds & Men*. Reserving brown for the lead bird's beak and eye allowed the artists to borrow it for the title band and oval without distraction. Its wings stretch further than nature meant them to go, but they do give a vivid impression of a bird on the verge of flight.

The lapwings on the jacket of *Farming and Wildlife* were inspired by the flocks that visited the winter fields below the Wiltshire downs close to the Ellises' home. Around this time, their daughter Charlotte had spotted a ploughed field covered with 'peewits'. She took Clifford to see them in her new, bright-green Citroën 2CV, but each time they stopped to allow Clifford to sketch the scene, the birds took off. It was the memory of the great flock of skittish lapwings rising from the stubble that seems to have inspired the jacket of *Farming and Wildlife*.

Clifford himself said of this scene that 'the birds themselves "know" about tone values. When they are on the ground they have v. little anxiety if you pass in a car. But if you are on foot you are dangerous, so they turn away and the white plumage (and the birds) disappear until they have run a safe distance; then they take flight, and white plumage reappears, and nicely visible, they are suitable for a book jacket' (CE to Libby Hoseason, 8.2.81).

67

Farming
and
Wildlife

KENNETH
MELLANBY

Farming and Wildlife

KENNETH MELLANBY

COLLINS

68   Mammals in the British Isles

L. Harrison Matthews, 1982

'Mammals 2' was an update of the classic New Naturalist *British Mammals*, published more than thirty years before. Remarkably, both books were by the same author, by now in his eighties. This time Leo Harrison Matthews chose to cover the field by topic rather than by species; the new book was discursive, review-like, and, above all, short – *Mammals in the British Isles* is only half the length of *British Mammals*.

Its jacket was among a batch of designs C&RE completed back in 1974, long before the book's publication. The colours are rich and bright, and the forms looser and freer than ever. Two young stoats are racing through a tangle of bramble, the rich, warm browns of the animals matched by the autumnal foliage. Perhaps they have heard the trilling call of their mother announcing she has caught a mouse and are racing to get there first. The surprise colour is the bright blue. It has no particular function in the design except as shadow, but it complements the brown unexpectedly and enriches the tones.

Jonathan Gibbs, writing in the *Financial Times*, thought the 'cutesy weasels' [*sic*] 'look as if they might be a detail from a medieval wall-hanging' and found the artists' 'Arts-and-Craftsy aesthetic' 'at once archaic and modernist'. This design is best appreciated at an angle, where the head of the leading stoat curls around the spine to complete the sinuous curve of its outline. The effect is spoiled once his poor, light-sensitive little head turns to pale brown.

68

Mammals
in the
British Isles

L. HARRISON
MATTHEWS

Mammals
in the British Isles

L. HARRISON MATTHEWS

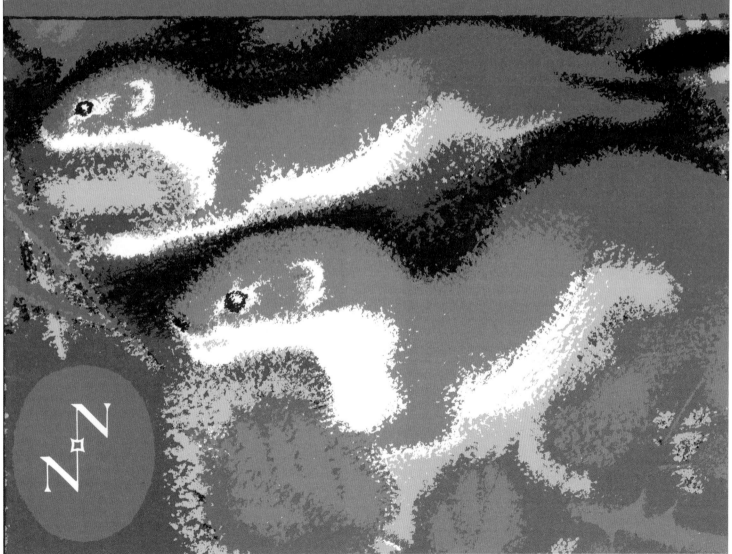

69   Reptiles and Amphibians in Britain

Deryk Frazer, 1983

ABOVE Artists' reference sheet for *Reptiles and Amphibians* with colours and selected Pantone numbers on note pad (15 × 10 cm).

Like *Mammals in the British Isles*, this book is an update of a classic New Naturalist title, Malcolm Smith's *The British Amphibians and Reptiles* (Deryk Frazer had taken the latter through several revisions after Smith's death in 1958, and so was the obvious choice for his successor). This book was the last in the series to be printed in the traditional text format. It was also the last-but-one Ellis jacket.

C&RE designed it in 1982. Having put a reptile on the jacket of the Smith book, they decided it was the turn of the amphibians and chose a common frog. The animal is in the water with just its head poking above the surface and the rest of its body reduced to a blurred pale green outline. The effect is rather comic. The lower half of the jacket is devoid of detail leaving the focus on the frog's head, plus a mish-mash of deeper tones above the deep green band. In response to a request for a reptile as well as an amphibian, the artists added a row of lizard spots to the spine.

'Your colleague's request for a reptile on the spine may be met by the placing there of an enlargement of part of the dorsal pattern of a Sand Lizard,' explained Clifford. 'This distracts less from the frog on the front than a representation of a whole reptile would be. Anyhow they are all too lengthy – as this soon will be. P.S. Nowadays everybody is familiar with reptile skin, real or artificial.' I wonder if this is true; I had always assumed the spots were meant to be frog spawn.

C&RE's penultimate jacket was published on shiny paper which does not suit it. The editor, Libby Hoseason, had asked the artists whether they preferred 'to show us your colour roughs first to spike the grumble-brigade's guns, or proceed direct to separations. Could you let me know?'

69

Reptiles and Amphibians
in Britain DERYK FRAZER

COLLINS

70   The Natural History of Orkney

R. J. Berry, 1985

OPPOSITE Variant design of *Orkney* jacket, full size, gouache and pencil on watercolour paper.

Orkney and *Shetland* are, in effect, companion volumes (though *Orkney* is also often paired with *Warblers* as the first two books with a paperback edition, and also as the two rarest and most expensive hardbacks in the series). They are by the same author-editor, Professor 'Sam' Berry, and have the shared stated aim of relating the natural history of the islands to their rapidly changing economic circumstances. Both books were sponsored by North Sea oil giants, in the case of Shetland by BP, for Orkney by Occidental Oil. But, after his experiences wrestling with a multitude of authors for *Shetland*, Berry decided to write *Orkney* alone, 'as Winston Churchill wrote his books: commission individual chapters from experts, and then re-write them into a flowing whole'.

For their last jacket for the New Naturalist library, Clifford and Rosemary Ellis drove all the way to northern Scotland where they caught the ferry to Orkney; their trip, made in late summer 1983, was sponsored by Occidental Oil to whom Clifford afterwards presented an invoice for £205. Among other things they sketched and photographed North Ronaldsay sheep 'feeding on kelp torn loose by storm and exposed at low tide'. Not content with that, Clifford sketched more Orkney sheep at the Rare Breeds Survival Centre in the Cotswolds.

Sam Berry had 'a panic' when he saw the roughs of the jacket as the sheep's face was shown as white, and not their usual pale-brown. But after enquiry he was assured that their faces go white by the end of winter, and that some are that way all year round, 'so the cover is fine'.

Is the cover fine? It is certainly ingenious and economical with colour; the bright green (perhaps too bright?) of the title band is otherwise used only for overlaps. The top register with terns flying along the coast is pleasing, and the colours are soft and pleasant to the eye. But the central character, the sheep facing us, doggedly chewing its fragment of weed, seems oddly flat and two-dimensional, curly ram's-horns notwithstanding. On the 'colour separations' of the artwork the effect works splendidly, but somehow the charming features of the sheep were lost in

179

translation. The 'rough' of the jacket was hung on the wall of Crispin Fisher's office at Collins.

This is, perhaps, a jacket for the connoisseur. It is also a jacket for the rich, for Fine copies of *Orkney* have fetched up to £2,000 in recent book auctions. The full design was confined to the tiny hardback edition of only 725 copies (plus 500 rebound copies with laminated jackets); the paperback distorts the design by omitting the spine and its crucial completion of the ram's horn, while printing it on inappropriate glossy boards.

Orkney is also, in retrospect, a sad jacket, for it was the Ellises' last completed design for the series. Clifford and Rosemary Ellis had designed 86 jackets over nearly forty years. Clifford's death, in March 1985, aged 78, after a short illness, was therefore the end of an era. Rosemary was invited to design the next jacket, for *British Warblers*, alone, but declined. 'Reluctantly I am writing to say that at the moment I have not the courage, the heart or the time to undertake the jacket,' she wrote. 'I am sad about this as the New Naturalist books are part of my life.' Crispin replied that their work had been part of his life too: as the son of James Fisher, they had been part of his upbringing. 'Your work has a freshness and quality as modern today as it was 43 years ago,' he added, 'and that can't be said for any other graphic designer I know.'

This might have been the moment for a radical redesign of the series in favour of the photographic jackets so long hankered for by some of the editors. To his eternal credit, Crispin Fisher saw absolutely no reason to change. He had no doubt, either, about whom he wanted to take over the task of producing jacket designs for the series.

Over to you, Robert Gillmor…

The Jackets by Robert Gillmor

Introduction

OPPOSITE The artwork for *The Hebrides* was drawn in black ink on four plastic sheets, one for each colour. Overlaps were planned to achieve extra colours and here the blocks for yellow and grey overprint to produce a dark ochre colour.

WHEN ONLY TEN YEARS OLD I became aware of the New Naturalist series, although at that age I was quite unaware of its significance. The second volume, *British Game*, was among the books in my grandfather's library. I would pore over them on frequent visits, as my grandparents lived only a couple of easy cycling miles away. I also loved to spend time in Grandpa's studio, watching him slowly and carefully printing his colour woodcuts, all by hand, using the traditional methods of Japanese masters. Collins had sent him a complimentary copy of *British Game* as it contained a reproduction in colour of his painting *Blackcock lekking*. In pencil he had corrected the caption, as it was not, as stated, an oil painting, but a watercolour painting on linen.

But that was not the principal attraction of the book for me. It was the dust jacket, filled with a huge Grey Partridge, running towards the spine, but with its head, appearing above the title band, turned back, the eye and beak giving it a hunted expression. Almost abstract shapes of flying birds enlivened the spine. The colours were simple; terracotta, grey, a pale yellow green and a very dark brown. Where the grey overlapped the yellow green, a darker, olive green resulted. The initials and numbers in the bottom right-hand corner, C&RE 45, meant nothing to me. But the life and vitality of the speeding bird, the colours and textures, made an impression which turned into a lifelong passion for the work of the remarkable couple who gave the series its unique, distinctive and instantly recognisable appearance.

Nearly forty years later, in April 1985, I was attending the annual conference of the BOU. Crispin Fisher, a friend and fellow artist, then at Collins editing the New Naturalist series, buttonholed me over the weekend. Clifford Ellis had died earlier in the year and Rosemary felt she could no longer carry on with the series they had created so many years before. Crispin wanted me to 'take over the mantle of the Ellises' and 'become the designer of the jackets of all future New Naturalist titles which we publish, until further notice.' I was both thrilled and appalled. How could

Y

Green.

I possibly even dare to take over such a commission, one that had achieved such iconic status and which I admired so much? Crispin was adamant, but I clearly did not immediately say 'yes'. He wrote straight after the conference, 'You asked me to put in writing the various proposals which I made to you on and off during last weekend at Exeter. Even though I realise that this request was just a technique for buying time on your part nevertheless I am happy to do so.' After detailing what was needed, including the snappy sentence, 'The first jacket we need is already urgent', he ended his letter 'Perhaps you would let me know as soon as you can whether you will take this series on for us. You already know that there is only one answer I will accept!'

What could I say, other than that I was truly, deeply honoured, and completely terrified at stepping into the shoes of two such great artist designers. Shortly afterwards I was tackling my first jacket, for *British Warblers* by Eric Simms.

I was already quite experienced in doing artwork using a few flat colours, mostly covers for BTO publications, annual reports, greetings cards etc and had experimented with overlapping to make additional colours, and had done this regularly when printing linocut prints. My own collection of NN volumes was fairly small, with most of the bird titles, the monographs and a few others which had come my way. John Steers' *The Sea Coast*, for instance, published in 1953, had helped with my A level geography.

I had long studied the Ellis covers, trying to work out the range of colours and sequence of printing. My favourites were the smaller monographs with deceptively simple, bold designs. *The Heron* was particularly successful, printed in only two colours. An opaque grey overprinted the black to create a dark intermediate grey. The same trick was performed on the cover of *The House Sparrow*, this time with three colours where the rich brown prints over the black for the background, and the grey prints over both, resulting in six colours and the white paper making the seventh.

So I knew that there would be four colours, one of which would always be black. I have written about producing the artwork for *Warblers* in the section that follows.

My first seventeen jackets were all produced in the same way, a method that meant there was never a single piece of colourful artwork. Instead each design consisted of four black drawings, to be turned into four plates from which the four colours were printed. Usually there would be a careful pencil drawing, in pure line, over which I taped a transparent plastic sheet. The area for a particular colour would be filled in with black Indian ink. When that was dry another sheet of plastic would be taped on top and the next colour drawn or painted on. And so on, twice more. By working carefully on the overlays the four blocks should, and usually did, register accurately.

A lot goes on before the 'careful pencil drawing', the finished design, is arrived at. Firstly a brief tells me about the content and theme of the book, and it may include a hint of what the editor or the author would like to see, occasionally much more than a hint! Having studied the brief, I start doodling, often on tiny two-inch rectangles representing the cover, ideas for a possible composition. It is important at this stage to get something down, to make a start, even if these first thoughts are just that and do not survive even a few minutes. Those first doodles can lead me on, can show me a new direction or where not to go, or what may be worth exploring more thoughtfully.

Eventually a design emerges that looks promising and a tidier, full-size drawing is made, perhaps with colour added by crayon or felt-tip pens. This may become the drawing which I send to Collins, sometimes as my considered proposal, but sometimes I am less confident. Reaction can range from 'fine, go ahead' to 'we think that perhaps … etc' and I start doodling again. Usually it is somewhere in between, a tweak here, a small change there, and a fresh drawing takes wing to London.

Once everyone is happy I can go ahead, but not before the crucial measurement, the spine width, has been established. Word counts and the number of pages determine this, and as the cover is required at an early stage, there is often a delay before this magic number arrives. The cover is needed because it is used in pre-promotion, and I have sometimes been alarmed to discover that one of the preliminary sketches is being used for this purpose, despite its being far from the settled design.

Depending on the subject of the book, a good deal of research may be necessary. Authors can be very helpful in providing references, descriptions, and their own sketches and photographs. I welcome such input and try to accommodate what is suggested, although on occasions the author's idea simply will not work. Whilst I want the author to be happy, the overriding need is for a design that works on the cover, as a book jacket. It is not an extension of, or addition to, the illustrations inside.

In my book *Cutting Away*, I quoted from a letter written by Clifford Ellis, explaining why an author's ideas for a jacket were not entirely appropriate, which has in turn been quoted by Peter Marren. It is so apposite that I have no hesitation in repeating it once more: 'A book jacket is by way of being a small poster; it is part of the machinery of bookselling. Though, obviously enough, the jacket should be in keeping with the book it contains, it is unwise to consider it as an opportunity for an additional illustration. An illustration, as against the jacket, can be seen at leisure and free from the competition of not always very mannerly neighbours. The jacket should be immediately interesting; its forms and colours should make a very clear and distinctive image. If it does its job, the book will be taken down and opened, and the proper illustrations will be seen.'

The various stages in the production of an NN jacket can be summarised as follows. The brief arrives and I read through what has been sent. With a pad of blank paper, a doodling session will follow until a promising idea can be carried forward, enlarged and tidied up. This might become the coloured rough which I send to the editor, usually with caveats. A week or two later it will be returned with

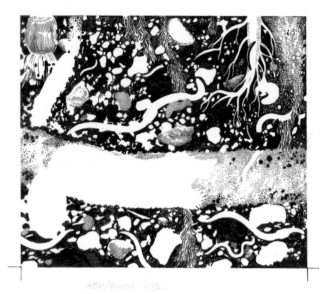

The artwork for the jacket of *The Soil*, drawn in black on transparent sheets, each with a Pantone number, and with lettering added to the green plate.

comments from the editors and perhaps the author. A fresh drawing may sometimes be necessary to accommodate their suggestions, sometimes not. There can be a swift progression to final artwork which is transferred to a lino block for cutting. Or there may be further delay and discussion before reaching the final stages. The first block that I cut will be the one with the most detail and, at this stage, I treat it almost like a drawing in lino, with all the areas of different colours delineated. I make a print from the block in black and place a new piece of lino precisely over the image before running it back through the press to offset the print onto the new block. I will do this on as many blocks as I think I am likely to need. Each block now carries the identical image, the right way round. I can now happily cut away, leaving the areas required for each colour standing proud. All the outlines on the first block, which are no longer needed, are cut away. Printing is from the raised, untouched surface, left once the 'background' has been removed. When printed together, the blocks should all register accurately.

Once all the blocks are cut they are ready for proofing. At this stage I have the colours and likely order of printing in mind, but the whole reason for the proofing stage is to get the colours right and establish the final order of printing. There is also the important business of cleaning up the blocks, cutting more away where necessary to improve registration.

I usually start with ten or twelve prints and print all the blocks so that registration, colour overlaps and colours in general can be checked. Occasionally

BROWN 472

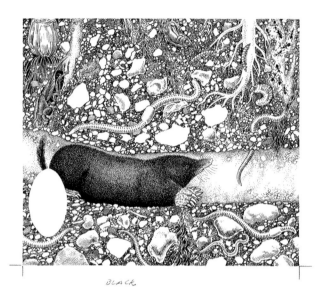

BLACK

pressure of time means that there is none left to do a new set of prints, and one of the first dozen has to be good enough to meet the deadline. Where needed, I can tweak a print, using a fine brush and the water-based printing inks as paints.

The colour of the title band is left until last so that I can choose a colour that goes with the print. I try to find a standard colour from the universal Pantone range, and give its code number which will be recognised from Norwich to Singapore.

Then the wait until the proofs arrive, when relief or desperation, acceptance or rejection, will result. Some proofs require little correction, others may need to be completely reworked. A telephone discussion will consider the proofs in detail and, unless a new set is demanded, all goes quiet, until weeks later when a heavy package is delivered and a crisp new volume is unwrapped. Even if the printing isn't quite what one had hoped for, it is always exciting to look through the new book, to examine the illustrations and perhaps dip into the text! But adding it to the line of books on the shelf, the latest in such a long and distinguished collection, is a moment to savour.

71 British Warblers

Eric Simms, 1985

ABOVE First thoughts for the composition.

BELOW Here I have used crayons, trying out possible overlaps of colour to see what might result.

Starting a new project can be fraught with all kinds of concerns, and working on my first New Naturalist, following in the footsteps of two designers whom I greatly admired, was, frankly, daunting. I was glad to start with a bird subject. Warblers are an attractive group, with many candidates for possible inclusion.

The tradition that I would follow used four flat colours which could be overlapped to make others. This restriction immediately reduced the possibilities. Blackcaps, the male with its bold black cap and the female with a brown cap, seemed a good start; but that used up two colours and I needed a green. By using blue and yellow, a green could be created. A Wood Warbler has a yellow front and the sky is usually blue, so the rest soon fell into place.

My first sketches had the male Blackcap on the spine, but as I was thinking of the importance of song in this delightful group of birds, I liked the idea of putting it on the front, large and in full song. The female would make a perfectly reasonable image for the spine. The green, made by printing the yellow over the blue, was not as strong as I would have wished, particularly for the leaves, but I was woefully inexperienced at this stage!

For the grey of the cock Blackcap I used a rub-down tint, made by Letraset. Their range of tints and rub-down typefaces was invaluable for much graphic work, although they were later made redundant by the development of computer programs.

At the time I did not realise that my first jacket would appear alongside *Orkney*, the last by C&RE, giving the NN enthusiasts an immediate comparison between our styles. Nor did we know that these two titles were published in such low numbers (725) that they rapidly became scarce and sought-after, and are now the Holy Grail of the dedicated collector.

British Warblers

Eric Simms

British Warblers

Eric Simms

72 Heathlands

Nigel Webb, 1986

For this jacket a selection of creatures and plants suggested themselves, but the colours presented quite a challenge. The end result was certainly colourful, dominated by the purple heather and yellow gorse. Blue and yellow again made green and the blue alone was strong enough for the Gentian. The purple, plus yellow, made orange. The lizard was green and yellow, and so on.

Unfortunately red and yellow are 'fugitive' colours and will fade rapidly when exposed to light for any length of time. For various reasons it is impractical to use light-fast inks for this kind of work, so the spines of many volumes have faded badly. Long ago I learnt not to use a yellow for the title band, since the white lettering soon becomes unreadable as the yellow fades away.

There has been speculation as to whether the setting for this design was based on a specific site, such as Hartland Moor or perhaps Purbeck in August? If the design recalls such places that is fine by me, but I was just reliving heathlands I have known, with no particular place in mind.

72

Heathlands

Nigel Webb

COLLINS

The New Forest

Colin R. Tubbs, 1986

73

This brought back many happy memories of summer holidays during and after the war. My grandfather had bought a tiny plot of land on the edge of the New Forest, near New Milton, where he put up a simple wooden hut with a verandah. All our holidays were spent there in just two rooms, one for living and cooking, the other with two beds. Before a second hut, with just enough space for two more beds, was erected, tents were the option for the junior members of the family. There were no services, the light coming from candles or oil lamps, with Primus stoves for cooking. The water came from a well, and you can imagine the rest!

I had not been back to the Forest for years, so this title gave me the excuse, not that I really needed one, to go and look up my childhood haunts. On those early holidays we went everywhere on bicycles, but now the car dominates and has been responsible for many of the changes that were immediately apparent.

Ponies, deer, bracken, great oaks and gorse-scattered common had to feature in my image of the New Forest. As for my bird, I added a Sparrowhawk in the top register. Sadly I could no longer include the Red-backed Shrikes that I remember watching forty years earlier on common land near Brockenhurst.

Mike Dilger, writer, naturalist and wildlife presenter writes: 'Trying to pick a favourite New Naturalist jacket is like trying to single out a favourite bird or plant; in other words, it's impossible. However, if someone were to twist my arm, I would probably say *The New Forest* – and it isn't even one of the sixty-odd that I own! In my opinion, all the New Naturalist jackets should be like the TV advertisement with that famous strap-line, 'it does what it says on the tin'. No better example is there than Robert Gillmor's design for *The New Forest* which captures the essence of the habitat in a single sumptuous image. If I imagine a scene in the Forest it is of a clump of orange bracken beneath a canopy of oaks, whereupon, peering between the gnarled old trees, I can see the common spreading out like the baize of a snooker table with New Forest ponies grazing in the distance. As I walk out of the trees for a closer look, a white hart scampers off when I tread on a dried twig … Good job it wasn't an adder!'

74 Ferns

Christopher N. Page, 1988

OPPOSITE This design, submitted to Collins, was drawn using felt-tip pens. These, although rather crude, are quite good at giving an idea of how overlapping the various colours will work. In this case there were very few changes to the final artwork.

I enjoyed working out this jacket. It was fun to find and then to arrange the variety of leaf shapes into a decorative design. The Horsetails, like miniature totem poles, provided a nice contrast to the curving leaves. They grew in profusion in an area of the garden that seldom saw the sun and from where I could pick them on the way into the studio.

I deliberately simplified the leaf shapes, omitting all detail. Two greens, an orangey brown and black enabled me to create three further colours with the overlaps.

Today, twenty years later, and having left Berkshire for the coast of north Norfolk, my wife has planted a collection of ferns under the printing-room window, joining others growing in the flint wall above. We love their elegant shapes and autumn colours which now ornament a permanently shaded area.

74

Ferns in the British Isles

CHRISTOPHER PAGE

75 Freshwater Fishes

Peter S. Maitland & R. N. Campbell, 1992

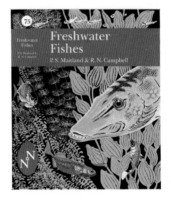

My first idea, the rough of which I carried out in some detail, featured a couple of Brown Trout in clear water, with Water Crowfoot and a Mayfly creating ripples to indicate the water surface. But the editors thought this was too specific and more suitable for a book aimed at anglers. So I thought again and chose a more colourful group from small Sticklebacks to a large Pike. Red-finned Rudd decorated the spine, and a couple of familiar freshwater pond weeds completed the design.

I am sure the editors were right to turn down the first idea even though I think it would have made an attractive cover, if not for this particular title. It demonstrates how important it is to get the cover right. In order to sell the book it must attract attention and instantly indicate the contents. It must encourage a potential buyer to pick up the book and look inside, after which the authors, designers, photographers and artists take over to make the final pitch.

The bright red was of course rather strong, especially for the Sticklebacks, but for an attention-seeking jacket which is not a field guide plate, I think it is justifiable.

The reworked design eventually produced the following from Myles Archibald: 'I have just received the authors' comments on the above jacket rough. Both authors liked the new rough and only had a few minor ichthyological comments, which I think are worth considering.' He enclosed a photocopy, annotated by Niall Campbell, with vital points I was glad to incorporate in the final artwork.

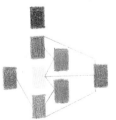

Robert Gillmor

First idea for Jacket of <u>New Naturalist</u> volume: <u>Freshwater Fish</u>

76 The Hebrides

J. M. Boyd and I. L. Boyd, 1990

I was rather happy with this jacket. Although I have never been to the Hebrides, I had visited the gannetry on Grassholm, an experience that still lives with me many years later. References were used for the view and, although it is not a precise configuration of islands, St Kilda enthusiasts will find aspects familiar! Then I had fun playing with the four basic colours, black, blue, yellow ochre and grey, and seeing what extra colours could be achieved by combining them (see page 183).

Like *British Warblers,* this is one of the rarer New Naturalist volumes, due to the very low print-runs of the first edition. Fine copies with undamaged and unfaded dust wrappers are much sought-after if and when they appear on the second-hand book market.

77

The Soil

B. Davis, N. Walker, D. Ball & A. Fitter, 1992

My first sketch showed two moles meeting in their tunnel, and presumably this must happen! But the reaction from above was summarised in a letter from Myles Archibald who wrote: 'The only minor points that you might need to take into account are that the *Soil* authors feel that there should only be one mole on the jacket (they are aggressive animals and never get close to each other).' Never?

I wanted to show that below the surface the soil teems with life. Worms, of course, but many other creatures as well. On the spine is a Mole Cricket, one of our largest insects, growing to 35 mm or more. Like the mammal after which they are named, they tunnel in the soil using their huge, strong front legs. Above the title band are plants, sending their roots deep down into the soil.

I was fascinated when Peter Marren pointed out that the jacket for the previous volume on the same subject, was a very much more austere design. In 1957 the Ellises had also been inspired by the mole, but simply showed its powerful foot, filling the space.

Black

409

78   British Larks, Pipits & Wagtails

Eric Simms, 1992

OPPOSITE The first composition idea for this title.

Of all my New Naturalist jackets this is the one I would most like to do again. The five main images are too small, and consequently I did not make enough of the strong patterns of the Pied and Grey Wagtails and the Shorelark.

I am sure I could make a better job of the composition now. The linocut technique would certainly lead me to a bolder design, with larger, stronger images. The colours are adequate and I would probably use similar ones again; but the feeble 'background', weak plants and pathetic indication of water lack conviction and imagination.

Presumably I thought it worked at the time, although there are preliminary sketches showing that the design had not come easily.

78

COLLINS

464

79 Caves and Cave Life

Philip Chapman, 1993

Caves and bats go together, and although there are many other creatures that live in caves, few cave dwellers are as well-known. So I chose a Horseshoe Bat, with its distinctive face, as a typical inhabitant of caves.

Of course I wasn't to know that only ten years later an NN on bats would come along. But I doubt that it would have stopped me featuring a bat in some way.

The illustration was drawn on Coquille Board, a material I had been introduced to by Al Gilbert, a distinguished American wildlife artist, when visiting the USA. It is a thin white board with a texture which is revealed when drawn on with a black crayon or Chinagraph pencil. It also takes pen and ink very well. The resulting texture is rather like that produced by the heavy limestone blocks which I used to print from in the lithography studio at art school. Each area of colour was filled in with black ink on sheets of transparent plastic, laid over the drawing to ensure accurate registration. This board is an ideal medium for rendering the soft fur of mammals.

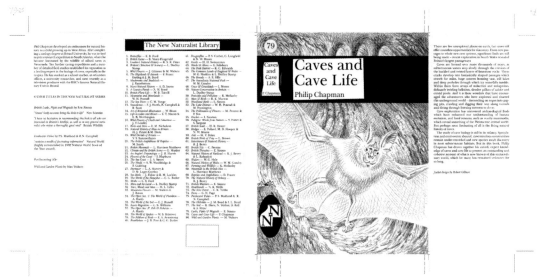

79

Caves
and
Cave
Life

P. Chapman

Caves and
Cave Life

Philip Chapman

80 Wild & Garden Plants

Max Walters, 1993

ABOVE I was working on this jacket during our annual holiday in north Norfolk, several years before moving there permanently, and made this sketch of honeysuckle which was growing in the cottage garden.

BELOW I submitted two compositions to the publishers which were colour photocopied and forwarded to the author for comment. He preferred A to B and added helpful notes. The red and yellow, on the title band and roses, were reversed, leading to the inevitable fading of the spine.

Honeysuckle and roses, wild and garden. A garden full of flowers and, outside the gate, the 'wild'. Originally I had a rose-covered arch over the gate, but I was asked to remove this as it partly obscured the view, such as it is, of what lies outside the garden.

Today I would not have used yellow for the title band as it is virtually impossible to stop the spine fading. The book would have to be re-covered, or placed in a dark place, to prevent the colour bleaching away.

Had I made it green I would have had to make the band on the next volume, *Ladybirds*, a different colour. I try not to allow the same colour to appear on adjacent volumes on the shelf.

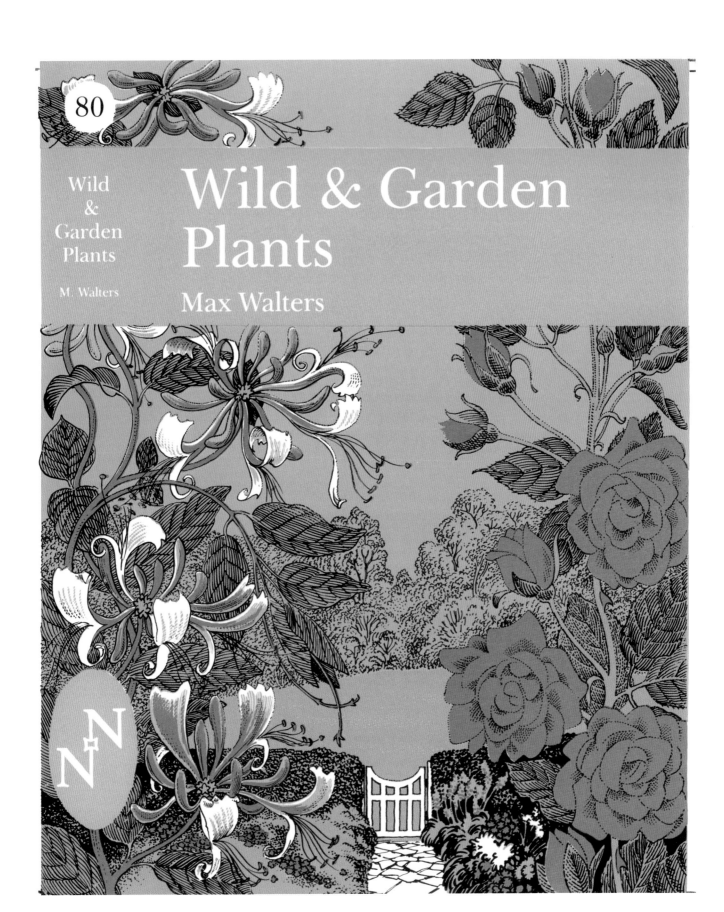

80

Wild
&
Garden
Plants

M. Walters

Wild & Garden Plants

Max Walters

81 Ladybirds

Michael Majerus, 1994

OPPOSITE The preliminary drawing was again drawn mainly in felt-tip pens and I evidently felt it was necessary to write a note at the bottom about the colours.

For me, there had to be a large, red ladybird dominating the cover. For Peter Marren ladybirds are small and dainty. He felt '…a huge one has elements of sci-fi'. He is right of course, but I have no regrets! The spine was just the place for a mass of hibernating Two-spots, crammed into a crevice.

As well as red, green and black, I used a yellow to alter the green in the background. It also gave me the possibility to include a yellow 22-Spot Ladybird as a contrast in colour and appearance, as well as a set of eggs placed on the leaf in the top register.

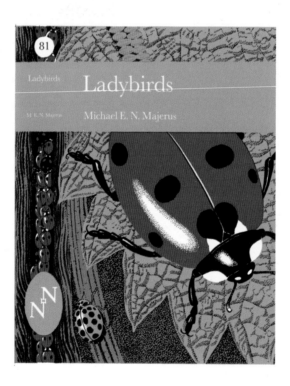

The colours here are far too crude. The red should be softer — more orange and the green more delicate. It is all rather rough here! Move large Ladybird slightly left — away from edge.   RG

82   The New Naturalists

Peter Marren, 1995, 2005

At first I agonised about how to illustrate the astonishing range covered by the series to date until, with a sudden flash of common sense, I realised that of course it is the books themselves that are the true stars. All collectors and lovers of the series like to see the serried ranks of matching spines on their shelves. A hand pulling out volume one from a mass of typical jackets, without any being actually specific, was my solution.

Knowing that the Ellises had drawn the lettering for *Butterflies* by hand, I determined to do the same, using their letter forms as far as possible. I followed their typographical style, with the author's name in large capitals, and the colours were also lifted from *Butterflies.* So, in many ways, this jacket was my tribute to the Ellises who had played such a significant part in the success of the series.

For the revised edition ten years later, I was asked to do a new jacket. The volume was to retain the same number as the original, but I wanted to do something quite different. I tried to imagine the desk of an author, not necessarily *the* author, but clearly a naturalist. The open notebook must surely belong to Sir Alister Hardy! The red Anglepoise lamp was my own, a gift from a good friend with whom I had spent much time sharing our mutual interests in birding and books. There are many other personal aspects of the picture. The Soay sheep skull was found during a school trip to Skokholm Island and it hangs above me as I write. On top of the bookcase is a decoy duck, brought back from a trip to the USA, and on the windowsill is a card based on a wood engraving of a hare by Charles Tunnicliffe, one of my heroes of wildlife art. The screensaver on the laptop is a detail of my linocut *Avocets, early morning.* There are several other personal items. A design like this is not one I would attempt as a linocut, and it was drawn in pen and watercolour wash.

The Ellises had, until the mid-1950s, decorated the NN colophon on the spine with a simple drawing relevant to the book's topic. I wanted to revive this admirable idea and drew a fountain pen, as the book is essentially about writers.

83 The Natural History of Pollination

Michael Proctor, Peter Yeo and Andrew Lack, 1996

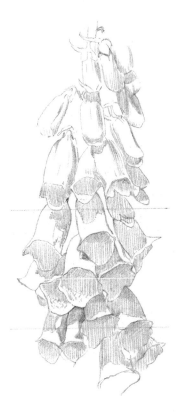

Perhaps a rather obvious choice, although entirely suitable to illustrate the subject of the book. In the mid-1990s, in urban Reading, we did not have Foxgloves in the garden, whereas in our Norfolk garden today they are abundant. However, I had been impressed by the imposing stands of strong, pink Foxgloves on Skomer Island where I spent nine springs studying the seabirds, and they were my inspiration.

At the time I was not familiar with the Ellises' design for volume 40, *Bumblebees*, where they have a very different approach to the same idea, showing the bee head-on from within the flower.

The authors made several very helpful and practical suggestions, including a request to change the species of bee. My first draft showed *Bombus terrestris*, but they pointed out that *B. hortorum* occurs more frequently on Foxgloves.

I particularly appreciated a paragraph in a letter from Michael Proctor. After discussing the 'jizz' of the bees he wrote: 'The important thing is to get the general impression right – or at least not to get it wrong in a way likely to jump to the eye of the bumblebee enthusiasts! Nobody is going to worry about finer points of anatomical detail. A nice "happy" eye-catching cover is what matters most.'

Exactly.

83

The Natural
History of
Pollination

Proctor, Yeo & Lack

The Natural History of Pollination

Michael Proctor, Peter Yeo & Andrew Lack

N·N

84 Ireland

David Cabot, 1999

My main experience of Ireland is based on several trips to Cape Clear, off the southern tip of Ireland. In the 1960s I used to go there with friends who were setting up a bird observatory on the island.

The view on the jacket is not a specific one, but I hope it says 'Ireland', and the liberal use of greens is no accident! The Hooded Crow, Choughs and Kittiwakes are all birds to be seen along the Irish coast. Looking at the design now, I am annoyed by the way the coastline and the top of the crow's head coincide so closely. Why couldn't I see that at the time?

This was my 'fattest' volume to date. The 'spine width' is all-important when working on the designs, particularly for the final artwork. Progress is often delayed until I receive the definitive measurement.

84

Ireland

David Cabot

Ireland

David Cabot

Plant Disease

David Ingram & Noel Robertson, 1999

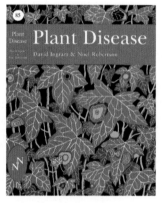

OPPOSITE It was hardly necessary to complete the rough sent to Collins, the right-hand side says it all.

This was a subject that I knew nothing about, so the briefing papers from the editor were all-important. As I read through the introduction and sample chapters, a slight feeling of panic crept over me; then the words 'Target Spot Disease', on ivy, caught my attention. There is ivy everywhere, so I went out of the front door and crossed the rough, unmade lane to examine the ivy on the flint wall surrounding the bungalow opposite. There it was, surely, it must be, brown and cream circles, whorls, spots and brown semicircles round the leaf edges. A great variety of shapes and patterns which could only be Target Spot Disease. Almost immediately it was clear how I would carry out the design – an overall pattern of ivy, with a selection of afflicted leaves beginning to take on a beauty of their own. I scurried around, excitedly collecting leaves with different patterns, some where the disease had eaten away circles just leaving the thicker veins holding the leaf together.

The limit of four colours was no problem. Brown, ochre, dark green and black for the background were enough, and the brown worked well for the title band.

From an anxious start, with no idea what to do, the design became a real pleasure to carry out.

86 Lichens

Oliver Gilbert, 2000

Churchyards, so rich in many aspects of natural history, are particularly good places to look for lichens and I was spoilt for choice locally. Remembering some especially striking examples on the tombstones around the ancient Priory at Binham, I went to investigate, and was not disappointed. Here were overlapping spheres of orange, white and grey, the only problem being which to draw and which to ignore.

The glassless windows of the ruined part of the priory led me to place the volume number in an orange circle against the white sky, one of the few volumes not to have a white disc for the number. Afterwards I wished I had used a tone over the sky and so retained the white disc. This would also have given the white lichens in the foreground more punch. It was not until the following year that I started to use tints to gain a wider range of tones and colours.

Not everyone has spotted the tiny black-and-white moth, beautifully camouflaged against the lichen.

Amphibians and Reptiles

Trevor Beebee & Richard Griffiths, 2000

ABOVE Sketches of a frog, the bottom one of which I used for the eventual composition.

BELOW LEFT Some of the pencil doodles made while trying to come up with a suitable design.

BELOW RIGHT When a design is finally agreed I make a key drawing in line over which the sheets of transparent plastic are taped. The four colours are then filled in over the appropriate areas.

My first idea was to include several different species, a snake, a lizard, a newt, or frog etc. Myles Archibald, in a telephone chat, didn't think it important to try to incorporate as many species and felt it was better to concentrate on the design. I also was not happy with what I had sent him and, as usual, simplicity was much more satisfactory. I tracked down some old sketches of a frog and placed it in front of a mass of frogspawn. A few strands of pondweed added a contrasting colour, unifying the main picture with the top register where they gave a shoal of tadpoles something to swim around. The adder on the spine survived from my initial design.

While I was working on the jacket I was unaware of the two previous volumes in the series on amphibians and reptiles, published in 1951 and 1969. In the first the Ellises had drawn a single adder winding its way across the front and up the spine. In the second they had also chosen a frog, mostly underwater with its head breaking the surface.

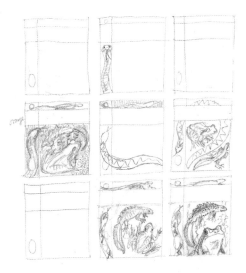

Amphibians
and Reptiles

Trevor
Beebee
and
Richard
Griffiths

Amphibians and Reptiles

Trevor Beebee and Richard Griffiths

88 Loch Lomondside

John Mitchell, 2001

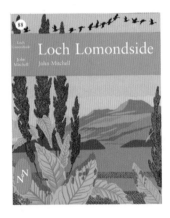

OPPOSITE John Mitchell was sent a crude colour photocopy of my rough proposal. For this I had used coloured crayons which are themselves rather crude. It is difficult to match the smooth depth of colour obtained by good colour printing. However, John was able to see past the colour and made a number of helpful points which he wrote in red on the photocopy.

The author, John Mitchell, was very helpful when he made a couple of suggestions for this jacket. He wrote 'The most important thing for inclusion to my mind is the unmistakeable and world-famous silhouette of Ben Lomond. From a natural history point of view, then, it is the Loch Lomond Dock which is unique to the area.'

Once I had submitted my rough he again made useful comments, pointing out that the flowering heads of the Loch Lomond Docks in my sketch were '...far too lax. The overall head to each plant should be more compact.' Such specialist knowledge is enormously valuable and I have been very grateful to many authors who have pointed out where I have revealed a lack of such knowledge!

They are the experts, and the authors, and I am only too keen that they should be happy with my attempts to sum up, in graphic form, the content of their work. Work which may have been at the forefront of their lives for years, decades or even a lifetime. Of course I cannot always express precisely what an author would wish; and then again there are others who are only too happy to leave it to me.

NW

88

For evening light,
very slightly lighter this
shadow &
darken this
shadow

Continue the western
outline of Ben Lomond
to separate it from Ben
Varlich in the distance.

Black tint   grey

Pale orange tint

SE

Flower heads too orangey & too lax

89 The Broads

Brian Moss, 2001

BELOW LEFT This was a preliminary idea, not submitted, before I decided on the message I wanted to convey on the cover.

BELOW RIGHT A print from the lino block cut for the black printing.

This was the first jacket artwork in which I made use of a linocut block, cut just for the black printing. The other three colours, and their tints, were drawn on transparent plastic sheets, exactly as for all the previous jackets.

This is about the only time I felt strongly that a more 'political' message should be conveyed through the jacket design. The spine and left-hand side of the front is in full colour and shows examples of the wildlife which once flourished on the Broads, a 'harmless' sailing boat in the distance.

The colour fades to grey and black, except for a jarring red on the speeding motor launch, churning up the waterway. I was trying to show that the Broads are perhaps heading for an uncertain future as they are increasingly taken over for leisure activities, careless of environmental considerations. Peter Marren put it very well: 'I thought the message was that misuse, symbolised by the powerboat, strips the biodiversity, exchanging colour and life for a grey murk.'

The Broads

Brian Moss

The Broads

Brian Moss

90 Moths

Michael Majerus, 2002

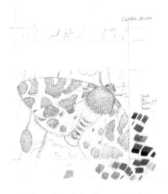

The first sketch before I tilted the moth away from the right-hand edge in order to make a more striking area on the spine and to bring the wing tip into the top register.

This design was hardly changed from my first doodle. Of all the wonderful and colourful varieties of moths, the Garden Tiger has one of the most striking and graphic patterns of colours and shapes. It is a gift to the designer.

The chosen colours, black, red, yellow and brown, allowed me, with tints, to create a range of strong colours. The red and yellow made a deep orange. The yellow, printed with a fine tint of the black, made the olive green for the background.

In a way this was one of the most straightforward jackets and I can only wish that there were more titles that gave me the chance to play with a truly bold and simple design.

Tints gave me the opportunity to expand the range of colours and tones, while still keeping to four colours, one of which was always black. The tint breaks the solid area of colour down to a fine, regular pattern of dots, best seen with a hand lens. According to the percentage of dots, from 80 per cent (darkest) to 10 per cent, the colour will be nearly as dark as the colour when printed solid, to a very pale version of the colour with more widely spaced dots. Even then it is not easy to see the individual dots. I would draw the area of colour in solid black and then specify the colour and percentage tint, making use of a fat book showing the tints available for each colour in the Pantone range of printing inks.

I had to visualise what would happen when the tints were overprinted and my experience as a print maker was a tremendous help. I could not always tell exactly what colour would result, but fortunately there were no disasters.

Nature Conservation

Peter Marren, 2002

ABOVE Sketches working out a pose for the Large Copper Butterfly.

BELOW One of the early sketches which were too muddled, although the Lapwing clung on to the end.

A broad subject like this is not easy to convey in a simple image, and several ideas were explored. Finally I settled on a tract of English countryside with a few readily identifiable creatures that rely on traditional habitats so often under threat.

I wanted to include a Lapwing as it is such a distinctive bird and its bold black-and-white plumage is particularly suitable for such a design. The remaining species are all of conservation interest. The Skylark is declining, the Kite has been successfully reintroduced, and the Harvest Mouse, Sand Lizard and Large Copper Butterfly are all beset with problems of habitat loss and degradation.

This was the second jacket where I used a linocut for the black printing, with the areas of colour and tints drawn in black on transparent sheets. Who has noticed where I missed out scraps of yellow which should have turned the two small areas of blue under the butterfly into the dark green?

I was so keen to see the Lapwing's head on the spine, that I did not consider carefully enough how this would affect the look of the front of the book, when the spine was not seen clearly. A headless Lapwing is the result.

On the softback editions, the original photographs did not wrap round onto the spine. Once my artwork began to be used for both hard and softback editions, I made sure that the spine, although still part of the whole, could nevertheless be omitted without ruining the design.

228

Nature
Conservation

Peter
Marren

Nature Conservation

Peter Marren

92 Lakeland

Derek Ratcliffe, 2002

As described, the early sketches had the Peregrine far too large. The final design hardly changed except for bringing the Wheatear in front of the Peregrine, so that it could be larger, and adding a Buzzard at the top. I brought the Raven into the main area on the front and added its mate for an aerobatic display.

I was so enthusiastic about including a Peregrine Falcon, that in the early sketches for this title the bird was drawn far too large, unduly dominating the jacket. Derek Ratcliffe took great interest in the development of the design and agreed, in a letter, that the first Peregrine was too large. He continued: 'Here are a few transparencies of Falcon Crag above Derwentwater, which was the kind of setting I had in mind. Two of them are too dark to show anything but the general scene. I leave you to judge how close the crag should be.'

This was the fifth design where I used tints of the basic colours to achieve additional colours and tones. The four main colours were black, purple, blue and yellow. The greens were achieved by overlapping tints of blue and yellow. Tints of the black and purple created other colours such as the rocks in the foreground and the distant hills.

The Peregrine and the Raven were birds very much associated with Derek Ratcliffe, and they were to recur in his second book for the series, *Galloway and the Borders*, published five years later: an indication of his love of the British uplands and their fauna.

British Bats

John Altringham, 2003

93

We are very aware of bats where I live in north Norfolk, with Pipistrelles living in the roof above the studio where I print my linocuts. Resident Pipistrelles and Natterers are a constant source of despair and irritation to those responsible for the care and cleaning of our great church, built when the village was once a major port. It now dominates a very different landscape reclaimed from the sea.

The church on the jacket is actually in the next village, but less than a mile from ours, no longer separated by a wide arm of the sea. Fortunately it does not have the same 'bat problem'.

Years ago, when illustrating the *Handbook of British Mammals*, my studio was full of boxes and cages containing a variety of small mammals modelling for my drawings. This mini menagerie included a Pipistrelle which fed enthusiastically on mealworms as I held him in my hand.

In my initial sketches the bat was stretched out like a pinned-down butterfly in a cabinet. The church also varied in size but gradually the composition developed into the final version.

British
Bats

John
Altringham

British Bats

John Altringham

94 Seashore

Peter J. Hayward, 2004

ABOVE More doodles as I played around with ideas.

BELOW The black block was largely line and cut in lino. This formed the key drawing over which I drew the colours on sheets of plastic.

This was the third jacket making use of a linocut, just for the black. The ripples were drawn in black and reversed out of the printing plates by the platemaker. Three other colours, yellow, red and green, made up the quartet. Other colours are made up by overlaps and tints. For instance the grey is a 40 per cent dot tint of the black.

In her briefing letter, the then managing editor, Helen Brocklehurst, who had carefully nursed me through several titles wrote: 'I am enclosing Peter's synopsis, which should give you some indication of the scope and content of his work. When I spoke to him about the jacket he seemed keen on it showing perhaps an invertebrate and/or seaweed – I'd like it to clearly say "seashore" to the general reader, but without looking too clichéd, so perhaps it would be possible to combine a few elements. The synopsis should give an indication of the range of species he discusses.'

The illustration was very much a childhood memory of dabbling in rock pools, the epitome of summer holidays. As well as the crab and starfish, there are Barnacles and Limpets, Beadlet Anemonies, Flat and Edible Winkles, and the seaweed is Flat Wrack.

Having spent considerable time and trouble cutting the black line block, it seemed a pity, even a waste, not to make further use of it. By cutting four more blocks I was able to turn it into a small linocut print, titled *Rock Pool*. All jackets since *Seashore* have been full-colour linocut designs, using, in some cases, very many separate blocks.

94

Seashore

Peter J. Hayward

Northumberland

Angus Lunn, 2004

95

OPPOSITE The first idea overdid
the emphasis on birds.

This key drawing shows the
numerous changes.

The original linocut
incorporated the title bar
and oval.

The first jacket proof shows the
county boundary before it was
inexplicably moved to the right.

So far, this is the only title in the series to deal with an individual county; a county with a rich variety of habitats, flora and fauna. In order to convey this I opted for a non-realistic approach, but one I hoped would encompass the wide biodiversity.

I was determined to include St Cuthbert's Eider Ducks, and the Black Grouse made a strong image for the spine. However, my first thought, inevitable I suppose for someone regarded as a 'bird artist', was to put a large Ring Ouzel on the spine, and give greater prominence to the Eiders and less to the Grey Seal. The editor pointed out that the birds were taking on too great an emphasis, not reflected in the text. So the ouzel was banished, the seal and ducks reversed and the Guillemot reduced in size. The sheep and another flower, Cloudberry, were also added.

As it was the first book on a county, and as I wanted to connect the disparate elements in the design, I thought that an outline of the county boundary would link them. The line was drawn separately and placed perfectly on the first proof. On the final printing something happened and I sent a grumpy letter to the editor:

'In making the plates the outline county boundary has been moved to the right by 4mm. This may sound trivial, but I had been extremely careful to arrange the design within the white line which now chops right through the head of the Blackcock, no longer neatly skirts the butterfly and pink flower heads and cuts into the head of the seal. [A reader] might well think that the designer was careless.'

There were two firsts for me with this jacket. It was the first I did as a full multicoloured linocut print and it was the first to be printed abroad. Previously I built up an excellent relationship with the Reading and Norwich printers. We did the whole job in a morning and I could pass the colours on the spot. With the move abroad, Collins requested 'camera-ready artwork' which meant that I could no longer send a set of black drawings, one for each colour or tone, to be put together at the platemaking stage. Now I had to produce a complete picture which could be photographed and transmitted round the globe to the printer. Popping over to Thailand was not quite as easy as the forty-minute drive into Norwich.

95

Northumberland

Angus
Lunn

Northumberland

Angus Lunn

N

Collins

96 Fungi

Brian Spooner and Peter Roberts, 2005

ABOVE As I live next to a Beech wood my first idea had concentrated on fungi likely to be found there, but of course this did not display the vast range of fungi covered in the book. A re-think produced a far better jacket!

BELOW The original linocut.

The linocut for *Fungi* was a real joy to research and carry out. My first rough was rightly criticised for having too many agarics (toadstools) and did not adequately reflect the broad content of the book and the rich variety of fungi which add so much interest to an autumn walk in the woods. Their names alone are an additional joy. Puffball, Stinkhorn, Porcelain Fungus, Amethyst Deceiver and Death Cap, with Peacock's-tail on the spine.

As with *Northumberland* I had incorporated the title band and logo oval into the actual linocut, something I now regret as it means I cannot reprint the designs as limited-edition prints. If I trimmed off the left hand side to remove the oval, the small bracket fungus creeping up the spine would be lost. This was based on fungus sprouting round the base of an old apple tree growing in the garden when we moved into our Norfolk cottage. It was already on its last roots and, after a year or so, died and eventually had to be removed. But not before the delicate little brackets had spread up the trunk and given me the idea for the spine. I also used them as decorative elements in a linocut print of a Great Spotted Woodpecker. A pair used to come to the tree searching for insects and their grubs, found in the dead and peeling bark.

When dedicated collectors of the series opened *Fungi* they were surprised to find a new look. Not just clean, new typography, with two colours on the title page and chapter openings, but colour throughout. Sadly, the coloured capital letter that opened each chapter only lasted for a few volumes. There were no longer clumps of colour photographs, but the photos were scattered through the text, a real improvement. With over 500 pages it was the longest volume since *Ireland* and the first of a series of heavyweight books, with even longer ones to follow.

We revived the illustrated colophon on the spine, but that was also abandoned after six volumes.

Fungi

Fungi

Brian Spooner and Peter Roberts

Collins

97 Mosses & Liverworts

Ron Porley & Nick Hodgetts, 2005

OPPOSITE The original linocut.

BELOW When working on a linocut I make a tentative order of printing. The first proofing stage shows whether the blocks register correctly and is also a chance to try out the likely colours and their relationship to each other. Sheets such as this result, as I use a finger to smudge on possible colours and their tones. On the right the final order of printing is listed, showing that nine separate printings were required.

The New Naturalist series covers such a wide range of topics that few scientists, and even fewer artists, can be familiar with them all. So the designer has to be prepared to cope with subjects about which he or she knows virtually nothing. This is actually one of the most rewarding aspects of the job and I enjoy the challenge of swotting up and finding out about something quite new to me.

It was clear from the start that I would need to enlarge these minute plants a great deal. Often the author can be a considerable help in providing ideas and references. I was captivated by the exciting shapes and colours that Ron Porley introduced me to and which I could incorporate into the design. I particularly liked *Polytrichum piliferum*, in the foreground, and *Pohlia nutans*, their red inflorescences and stalks providing extra colour and a variety of shapes.

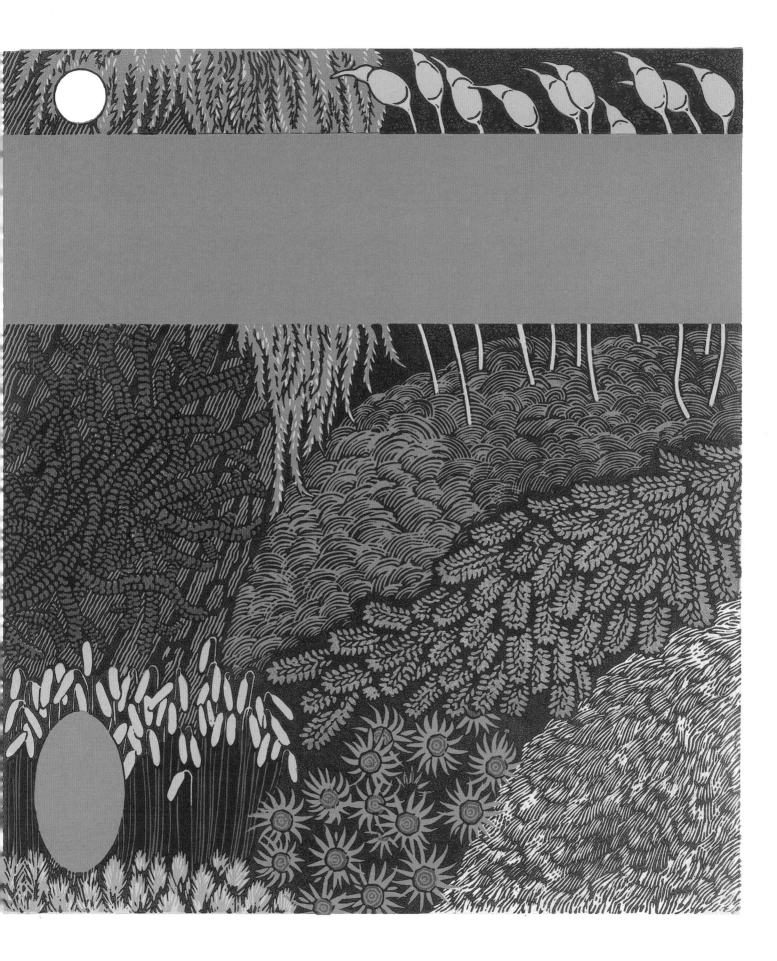

98 Bumblebees

Ted Benton, 2006

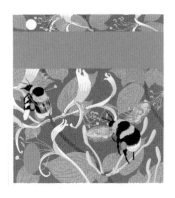

ABOVE The original linocut with possible colour for the title band added, using a coloured paper.

BELOW LEFT Although I was clear about the subject for this jacket, the details of the composition took several sketches before it was finalised.

BELOW RIGHT When drawing the colophon I do it as a negative – the pale parts in black – so that when it is reversed out of the oval, the dark and light tones will be the right way round.

I had only to step out of my studio into the garden to find the setting for this jacket design. A typical Norfolk flint wall runs the full length of the garden, but is virtually hidden by a great growth of honeysuckle. During the late spring, summer and autumn, this is a well-attended restaurant for a multitude of insects. Bees, butterflies, flies and moths, including the exotic Hummingbird Hawk Moth, throng to feed at the glorious white, trumpet-like flowers.

And that was it, some minutes looking and then collecting a few sprigs to draw, and the basic idea was settled. The elegant flutes of the honeysuckle made a pleasing contrast to the heavy, clumsy, bumbling bee (*Bombus hortorum*), with its furiously buzzing little wings somehow keeping it aloft.

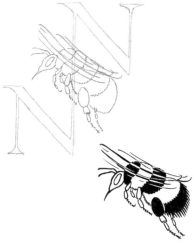

Bumblebees

Ted Benton

Collins

99 Gower

Jonathan Mullard, 2006

My only visit to Gower was many years ago, and I had little useful memory of the area visited. But a chance to make a trip came when Sue and I were staying in Gloucestershire while setting up an exhibition of my linocuts in the fine new visitors' centre at the Wildfowl and Wetlands Trust.

Jonathan Mullard had a clear idea of the view he would like me to consider for the jacket – Worms Head from Rhossili Down. He sent me a detailed map and off we went, heading for the western end of Gower where the narrow strip of land, Worms Head, stretches west. 'Worm' is a dragon, and it certainly looks rather like a vast, partly submerged dragon swimming out to sea. In the foreground we enjoyed the wide sandy beach of Rhossili Bay, and the cliff tops with their mounds of golden gorse. Jonathan wanted me to include the ponies which wander freely over the area. We came on a Stonechat, and that provided another splash of colour for the spine, in addition to the Yellow Whitlowgrass which Jonathan had suggested. Sadly, no choughs cavorted in the updraughts during our visit. The tight, rounded mounds of gorse, sculpted by the Atlantic winds, were a great contrast to the huge, untidy bushes of our Norfolk heathland.

We sat high on the Down enjoying a picnic and I made sketches and took some photographs. We had a close encounter with the large and superb Golden-ringed Dragonfly which let me approach within inches. A species of the west, not one to be seen at home.

This was the first volume to be wrapped in a different jacket paper. The earlier, coated papers allowed a more lively reproduction of my linocut prints, but on the new and more absorbent paper, the effect is much duller, as though, in this case, a thin mist has rolled in from the sea. The problem was to crop up again many times.

100   Woodlands

Oliver Rackham, 2006

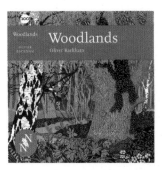

& reverse right to left

The hundredth volume in the series and my 31st jacket, having made different designs for the two editions of No. 82. As a linocut it turned out rather complicated, with ten separate printings.

The author, Oliver Rackham, had made several suggestions about aspects of the trees to be found in woodlands which might be considered. Rather too many to include all in the one design, but very useful nonetheless.

Naturally keen to include a bird, I eventually hid the first idea, a Pheasant, behind the oak tree and added a Jay instead. It seemed appropriate to include a bird responsible for extending the wood by its energetic, autumnal planting programme.

Dead Bracken, Bluebells and Primroses gave extra colours to add to the fresh yellow-green leaves of the Birch tree. Sadly, the reproduction on the hardback jackets rather lost the brighter colours of the original print.

ABOVE This was one of several early sketches in which I tried to incorporate some of the author's ideas. For the final design I found a more interesting way to treat the spine.

OPPOSITE The original linocut with the title bar printed on to show the colour I wanted.

101 Galloway and the Borders

Derek Ratcliffe, 2007

ABOVE One of the colour preliminary sketches was nearly there and much improved by replacing one huge Raven with two smaller birds.

RIGHT I have mentioned 'doodling' several times and this sheet is absolutely typical. Many, if not most, end up in the wastepaper basket but every now and again an idea appears which is worth running with.

Looking through my NN file I am now surprised to see how many preliminary studies I made for this jacket as I tried to find my way to a satisfactory composition. As with the previous book by Derek Ratcliffe, *Lakeland*, I started, like the Peregrine, with far too large a Raven. At first it was perched on a crag, beak open and obviously croaking loudly. A Peregrine flying past in the background, looking towards the Raven, appeared to have a surprised expression on its face, quite unintended, of course. The Raven moved around on its crag, getting smaller, but at last it took flight and was later joined by its mate. Meanwhile, a Golden Eagle glides into the top register and the Peregrine backs onto the spine and looks where it is going, no longer staring the viewer in the face. This may have been prompted by a letter from the editor which included the sentence: 'We're concerned about the Peregrine looking somewhat static with its head turned towards the reader, and think it would be good to have it in flight, as though heading towards the Raven.' All the while the background stayed much the same, although there was no cottage in the first few sketches. In the end the smaller images of the birds gave a better feeling of the wide-open landscape of Galloway.

This linocut was achieved with fourteen separate printings. There were four tones of green, two blues, grey and dark blue grey, slate and dark slate, yellow and brown. Pink and black made up the total. Really this is many more than I would use for one of my 'ordinary' linocut prints, but somehow the jackets seem to demand more colours, and this is by no means the greatest number that I have used!

101

Galloway
and
the Borders

DEREK
RATCLIFFE

Galloway and the Borders

Derek Ratcliffe

Collins

249

102

Garden Natural History

Stefan Buczacki, 2007

ABOVE The coloured drawing shows how seriously I took the first idea of including the 'attached dwelling place'.

OPPOSITE The original linocut, the title bar to be added at the platemaking stage.

The start of an NN jacket comes with the initial briefing, and the editor's letter of 12th September 2006 was typical: 'I have enclosed the author's synopsis, foreword and acknowledgements and chapters one and two. I have also enclosed a picture list which I thought might be of some use to you.'

While reading what has been sent I look out for something which might give me a clue as to the approach to take. Right at the start of chapter one Stefan Buczacki defines a garden and writes: '… that it is essentially a non-commercial undertaking; and second, that it is attached to or associated with a dwelling place.'

In chapter two he wrote: '… and my argument is that a large proportion of the population owns something attached to the building in which they live, no matter how small, and has done for at least 100 years.'

I was also impressed by what Stefan had to say about lawns, and I wanted to make a lawn the centre of my design. '… most gardens had at least a bit of grass, there are not only about 20 million gardens, but also about 20 million lawns.'

In the first sketches I showed a house at the top with lawn and borders attached. It was based, I must admit, on our own garden. I was also trying to indicate the man-made artificial nature of the garden. However, after a discussion with the editor, I abandoned the idea of 'attaching' the house to the garden and rather lost the obvious hand of man, except for a bird bath (later also discarded), but kept the sharp division of lawn and border and put more emphasis on the wildlife. In a letter I wrote: 'This still seemed to be getting very complicated so I zoomed in, reducing the plants and simplifying the design. At first I had a Blackbird pausing, looking for a worm, but I do like the idea of life happening in the garden, so restored the adult and chick. In lino it would all be simpler, bolder and more graphic.'

Simpler! This design eventually required sixteen separate printings.

I suggested, and drew, a design for the colophon incorporating a worm. Sadly, it was too late, as the decision to drop such decorations had already been taken.

103   The Isles of Scilly

Rosemary Parslow, 2007

The linocut print turned out to be one of the most complicated of the series with twenty separate printings, listed here in order of printing. The eagle-eyed will note that there is no red for the terns' bill on the list. Printing such tiny areas of colour would have been extremely tricky, not to mention cutting them in the first place. So I added them with a fine paint brush.

Once the artwork was completed, this jacket gave us all sorts of problems related to the reproduction of the vibrant colours in my linocut print. All who visit the Scillies speak of the light and tropical colours of the beaches and sea.

The view is an amalgam, an attempt to include several aspects of the islands into one view that would say 'Scillies', but not necessarily be specific. I had never been to the islands but many friends have, and one, Bryan Bland, gave me help and advice as my drawings developed. It was he who phoned from the airport, before leaving on one of his far-flung tours, with the brilliant suggestion that I include a Golden Oriole on the spine. It was just the dramatic splash of colour I had been looking for.

But the printers had the greatest difficulty in reproducing the various blues and greens that I had conjured from my tubes and bottles of lino printing inks. Even printing in six colours, instead of the usual four, did not really solve the problem. I had used twenty on mine!

It was lovely to be in touch again with the author, Rosemary Parslow, after many years, and she gave me great help and encouragement. She made valuable suggestions about the choice of plants and sent me photographs. In the first drawing I had nine terns flying across the scene, six over the near bay. The editors thought: '… it would be better to exclude the six terns flying over the sea (but to include the three at the top) so as to accentuate the vast blue quality of the water.' Rosemary wrote: 'Hope you can "save" the terns – I like the way they bring the design to life.' My compromise was to keep two of the six, but raised them to fly over the sky, under the title band.

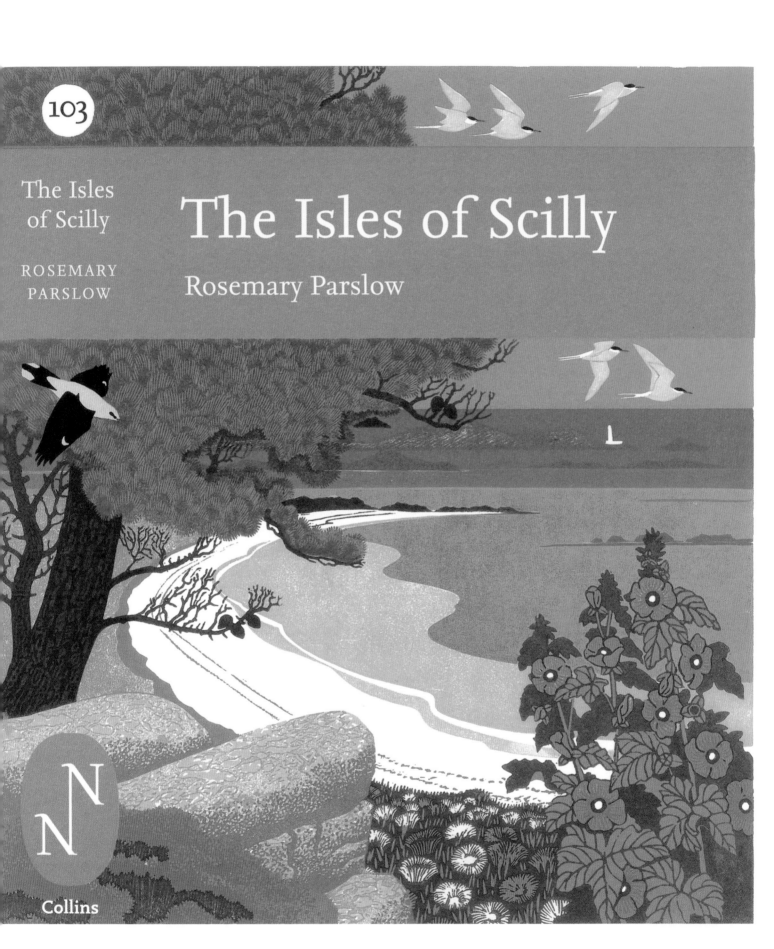

The Isles of Scilly

Rosemary Parslow

The Isles of Scilly

ROSEMARY PARSLOW

N

N

Collins

A History of Ornithology

Peter Bircham, 2007

ABOVE My first thought was to illustrate one of the naturalist clergymen, but it did not last long!

BELOW Two of the studies leading to the final artwork.

This was another title which produced masses of preliminary sketches and doodles before the final design emerged. I wanted to show how the history of ornithology lay in the published works of authors. Many of the early writers on natural history were country parsons, and one of my first ideas had such a clergyman sitting at his desk by a window, to his left a tall bookcase full of leatherbound books. On the desk were a couple of dead birds which he was examining. A flintlock rifle stood against the wall and, for the spine, a mounted bird stood on a cupboard. There were also blown eggs on the desk beside his inkwell and quill pen. Rightly, this did not find favour with the editors who, I soon realised, wanted to see some real, live birds on the cover. 'It occurred to me that perhaps a more abstract approach would indeed be more suitable. I know you are pursuing this route anyway, but it would be quite nice to see several interesting and striking birds on the cover, as this is probably what people will want to see!' Binoculars were also suggested and I was happy to include a pair. In addition I was determined to retain the flintlock rifle since this was used to bring the birds closer before the development of optical aids.

I was still hooked on the idea of books and did a number of drawings with birds, binoculars and the rifle, emerging from a background of shelves full of more leatherbound volumes. This didn't go down too well either. 'We are very happy with this more abstract approach, but slight amends to make it look less "bookish" would be great. Also, sketch c (Great Auk on spine) was very well received!' In the end I took the birds out into the countryside but kept a large open book.

The choice of species is pretty obvious. A bird now extinct, another lost as a breeding resident, two which have come here unaided and others being reintroduced. The binoculars were deliberately rather dated and I hinted at four distinct habitats. There are also a few personal nods to the past which I shall keep to myself! After all the work on the previous linocut for *The Isles of Scilly*, I was able to do this with half the number of colours.

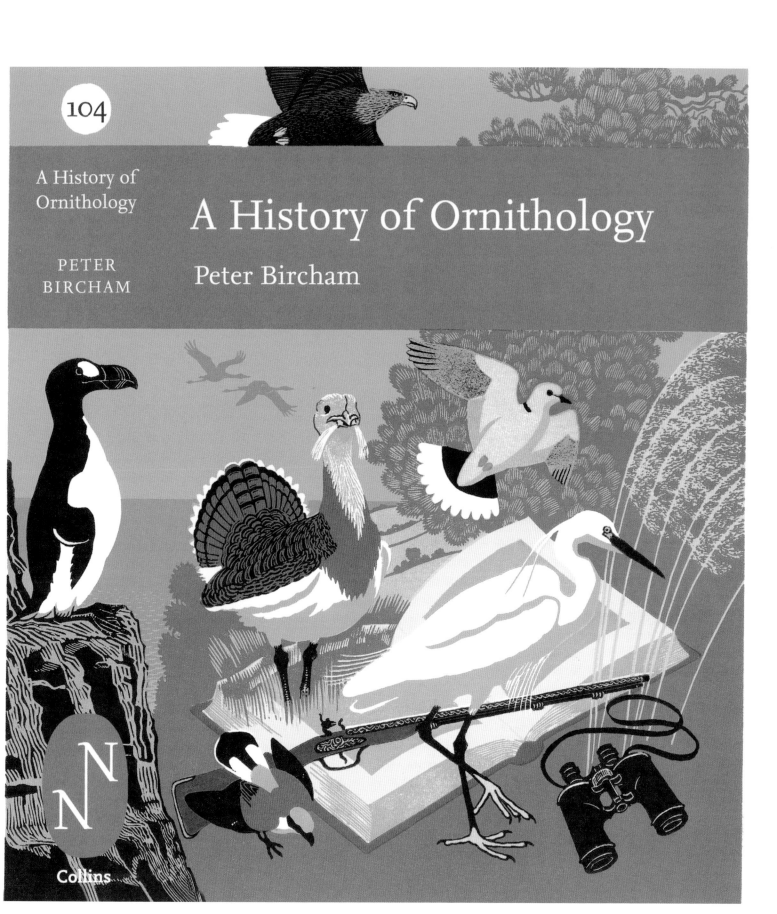

A History of
Ornithology

PETER
BIRCHAM

A History of Ornithology

Peter Bircham

N
N
N

Collins

105 Wye Valley

George Peterken, 2008

Another of George Peterken's comments on the first draft concerned the butterfly which was not resting comfortably on its oak twig. On this sheet I was trying to get it right and create an attractive spine.

This was another cover which gave the printers problems, and the author and I were disappointed with the final reproduction, particularly on the jacket of the hardback edition. All colours and contrasts have been lost in a mist which seems to have drifted in over the Wye.

The card covers of the paperback edition are different to the paper used on the hardbacks. The coated card does not absorb the inks as much as the paper, resulting in a brighter, more colourful and more accurate reproduction of the original.

As with others in the series, this is not a specific site on the Wye, but an attempt to capture the character of the area by bringing familiar elements together in one view. George Peterken, in an extremely helpful letter, written on sight of my first sketch, wrote: 'We are enthusiastic about the general design, which evokes the core of the valley very well, and we hope the final result will stay close to this draft. We have a few comments/suggestions on detail – the "we", incidentally, includes my wife, who has more of an eye to colour and tone than I have.'

He went on to make practical suggestions which I was all too willing to incorporate. He described how the Wye woods '… are more mixed than almost any other in Britain, so it would be appropriate to hint at this by introducing some variety into the crown shapes on the left slope – beech, oak, ash and lime would be the main canopy species.'

Another vital suggestion was his telling me about a Wye characteristic that I had missed: '… the emergent boulders in the main channel and the subsequent eddies in the flow. Is there any possibility to hinting at these?' Of course.

He finished his letter: 'Hope these comments are helpful. They amount to thoughts on how the existing design might be slightly more evocative of the Wye's natural and artistic history than it is already.'

His comments were certainly helpful and I was more than grateful for them, and all the more sorry that the completed result was not satisfactory for either of us.

Wye Valley

George Peterken

106 Dragonflies

Philip Corbet & Stephen Brooks, 2008

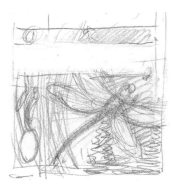

A couple of first thoughts. It was fortunate that I did not carry on with the bottom design. On seeing the first rough, Philip Corbet had pointed out that the Emperor keeps its body very straight.

I enjoyed doing this jacket, but there were some frustrations over timing and lack of communication between me and the authors, which was not our fault. Fortunately I was able to tweak the finished linocut print once I received Philip Corbet's detailed comments on my first rough sketch. In the circumstances he was extremely helpful and generous. I had already noted some points on that first very rough rough that needed attention, and which Philip was to comment on, before finally cutting the blocks for the linocut.

There were twelve blocks, including three greens and two blues. The final printing was the block for the wings of the Emperor Dragonfly on the front. I wanted to suggest movement, and also show the transparency of a dragonfly's wings, so the block was printed with a very thin film of pure white.

The colour of the title band was not as I had specified. As I wrote to the editor: 'I had asked for a much darker green which would have enhanced the other colours and broken up the top right corner. As it is, the band is almost the same colour as the background [on the hardback jacket] and the typography unfortunately lines up with the wing and sky, creating an empty rectangle.' In my complaining letter I went on: 'If the type had been the same length as on the paperback it would have worked more satisfactorily. On the paperback, the band has come out lighter than the background and, with the longer line of type, this problem does not arise.'

Philip Corbet and I had talked and corresponded at the end of January 2008 and it was a great shock to learn of his sudden and untimely death less than a fortnight later. I received a letter from the editor at Collins, who wrote: 'I am sorry he will not get a chance to see the final cover of *Dragonflies* – let alone the publication of his much-anticipated, definitive new book – though I know he was pleased to have seen his suggestions taken into account on the cover. Thank you again for accommodating this and for your help in resolving the matter amicably. I know that Philip was very grateful for this.'

106

Dragonflies

PHILIP
CORBET
&
STEPHEN
BROOKS

Dragonflies

Philip Corbet & Stephen Brooks

N
N

Collins

107 Grouse

Adam Watson & Robert Moss, 2008

In my first rough, done too hurriedly, I did not take enough trouble with the background, and this led the authors, very reasonably, to make a remarkably restrained comment, relayed to me by the editor. 'Their only comment related to the background/landscape, which reminded them both (independently) of the Alps rather than Britain. Seeing as our audience is mainly British, it would be worth bearing this in mind whilst preparing the final artwork.'

Quite!

We had the usual gripes when the proofs arrived about the difference in printing quality between the hard and softbacks but the end result was acceptable. The linocut had been straightforward, although I didn't manage to reduce the number of printings below fourteen, and half of these were greens and blues.

Grouse

Adam Watson & Robert Moss

107

Grouse

ADAM
WATSON
&
ROBERT
MOSS

N
N

Collins

108   Southern England

Peter Friend, 2008

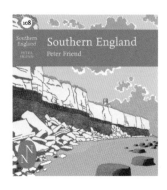

I have mentioned before how working on the series has brought me back in touch with old friends, some not seen for decades. In March 2007 a letter came out of the blue, with Department of Earth Sciences, University of Cambridge printed on the envelope, giving me no clue as to its sender. It read: 'I am a voice from the past, fifty years to be exact, when we coincided in Spitsbergen in 1957. You were with a four-man expedition from Reading, and I was with a four-man expedition from Cambridge. I remember somebody's birthday party in Skottehytta at the end of our visits, and I also remember visiting you in Reading after we had all got back to this country.'

It was my birthday party, my 21st. Our respective expeditions met up at the end of two months on Svalbard in a large trappers' hut, awaiting 'rescue' by the Governor's launch which was to take us all back to Longyearbyen. My birthday had been earlier in the trip but, with all the rest of our gear, we had lugged a wooden box around with us, on canoes and sledges, until it was finally broken open in Skottehytta. Inside was a present from Huntley and Palmers, the Reading-based biscuit company who had sponsored our expedition with tins of heavy and nutritious biscuits. The box contained a large cake, with pale-blue icing, decorated with polar bears and penguins! We had a great party.

After further reminiscences, the letter went on: 'I have also been working on the compilation of material for a book, *Southern England*, which is to go off to the publishers this week. You will understand why I am making contact at this point, when I say that the book is to be one of the New Naturalist series. I have not talked to Myles Archibald about this, of course, but I suppose that he may ask you to work on the cover jacket, as you have for recent New Naturalist books.'

It was good to hear from Peter Friend again, and in due time a briefing letter came with the manuscript of his book. Naturally I turned to the section on East Anglia, and areas in reach of home, in case there was something that would spark an idea. At first I had assumed that I would probably have to head south, to the Downs perhaps, but here was an account of the remarkable two-tone, three-colour cliffs at Hunstanton, less than an hour away round the coast. I had not seen them, but Peter's description was encouraging: 'Hunstanton is also famous for the three differently coloured layers of bedrock in its cliffs: a layer of Late Cretaceous white chalk overlies an Early Cretaceous layer of brown sandstone (Carstone), with a thin layer of red chalk between them. The detached and fallen blocks of white chalk at the base of the cliff show that the cliffs are collapsing and moving inland all the time. The regular rows of weed-covered Carstone blocks in the lower part of the beach show how the storm waves have created a wave-cut platform with a regular system of joints (cracks).'

So, early on a bright, breezy day in May 2008, I headed west and drove onto the vast car-parking area above the Hunstanton cliffs. I was virtually on my own, except for a distant dog walker. When I came down onto the beach for my first sight of these famous cliffs I was amazed and excited. Surely there was something here I could use. The striking clarity of the layers of bedrock beautifully illustrated the theme of the book which examines the underlying structure of southern England and how it determines the landscape.

BELOW
One of the sketches made when
I visited the dramatic cliffs at
Hunstanton.

Hunstanton
May '08

I made drawings, took photographs and watched the Fulmars flying up and down the cliffs, occasionally landing to cackle noisily with mate or neighbour.

On 21 May I wrote to the editor enclosing my idea for the jacket. My letter went on to say: 'We are deep into Norfolk Open Studios (until 1 June) with 100 people coming through on Saturday and 65 on Sunday. I have arranged a NN jacket exhibit in my printing studio and it has proved of great interest to numerous NN enthusiasts! We start again on Friday for four days and the following Friday for the final three.' By the time we finished, 600 people had been through the studios.

The question I am asked most is: 'How long does it take?' It is very difficult to answer, at least to the satisfaction of the enquirer. To say that a job, from receipt of the brief to the posting of the finished artwork, can take several weeks, or several months, may be true but is not quite what is required. It has to be explained that I do not work continuously on a job, from 9–5, six days a week. In order to extricate myself from lengthy explanations and discussion I might say that cutting for example seven blocks takes about a week. But a small area of colour, for instance the red wattles of a grouse, might take fifteen minutes; while work on a full key block could last for a few days. Even when fully into an NN jacket, other distractions, work or social, can take me away from it for short, or even long, periods of time.

Hunstanton May '08

265

109 Islands

R.J. Berry, 2009

The first sketch with the giant wren. The patrolling fulmar flew off in favour of a party of puffins whirring past.

With the briefing for this title came a note: 'Herewith some material for the next NN *Islands*. Myles and I had an initial chat and wondered if something like St Kilda field mouse and St Kilda wren, with the St Kilda high street in the background might work...? Good examples of island biology that feature prominently in the text, as you will see...Just a thought!'

St Kilda was an obvious but excellent choice. I was familiar with the well-known photographs of the strung-out houses and cleits, but I thought that as this was a book on islands the sea must be a major part of the design.

By a remarkable coincidence I had recently inherited the library of a dear friend, who was also a good naturalist, with a great interest in the Scottish islands. There was a shelf full of books, some very old, and all devoted to St Kilda, so I started my research in an upstairs bedroom, the only room left with space for a new bookcase! An early photograph gave clues to the view I wanted, although it did not include the cliff that appears on the spine or the rocks which provide a setting for the Wren.

A Soay Sheep made the sort of image for the spine that I look for, with some classic, island seabirds. My attempt to include the mouse didn't really work. The first sketch had the wren twice the size, but it was thought it might look too much like another book on wrens.

I managed to keep the number of colours to ten. There were actually eleven printings because it was easier to print the tricky little black wing tips, on the line of gannets, separately from the other black printing.

109

Islands

Islands

R. J. BERRY

R. J. Berry

N
N
Collins

To keep it bold and simple, with a limited colour range, I chose six almost black and white species for the original artwork, with small areas of colour. I needed a yellow for the beaks of the Whooper swans which, when printed over the blue watery colour for the background, would make a green – suitable for the patches on the back of the Eider's head. I planned to use the yellow on the title band, not then realising what a mistake that would be, as yellow would have faded badly.

110

Wildfowl

David Cabot, 2009

For nearly twenty-five years an increasingly tatty, brown, card-backed envelope has wandered around my studio. The postal label, dated 25 November 1985, advertises Alistair MacLean's *The Lonely Sea, Short Stories From the Master of Adventure*. Another, larger label, just carries the words Collins Publishers and the address, then 8 Grafton Street, London. Framing the label is a restrained, but decorative, border made up of a repeated, square leaf design. This, and the words, are printed in pale green and the whole is typical of the neat typography that I would have been doing myself, thirty years earlier in the printing department of my art school. Today, none of the correspondence from Collins addresses me as Esq.

The envelope would reappear occasionally, sometimes having escaped attention for a year or two, and I would take it out and look at the artwork within, certain that one day it would be needed. And, at long last, its day arrived.

When I started working on the NN jackets in 1985, one of the first designs required was for a book on British wildfowl. At that time the artwork was drawn for printing in four flat colours, with a little overlapping where possible to create additional colours. Wildfowl form one of my favourite groups of birds and I tackled the task with enthusiasm.

But, for various reasons, the book was delayed and the design put away in a drawer where it was gradually covered and lost to view for several years. Eventually, some forty titles later, *Wildfowl* was really on the way. By now I was doing full colour linocut prints and the only restriction on colours was how labour intensive I allowed it to be. There seemed to be no reason to change the original idea, except to brighten and enliven it with more colour. The Smew became a Merganser and the Tufted Duck a Pochard. The treatment of the water was simplified to go with the bold, unfussy handling of the birds. For the first time I made the main part of the jacket larger than usual and printed the band across the top, with the swans, separately.

110

Wildfowl

DAVID
CABOT

Wildfowl
David Cabot

N
N
Collins

nMn

Jackets by Clifford & Rosemary Ellis

1 The Badger *Ernest Neal, 1948*

A parallel New Naturalist series on single species or related groups of species was already under active discussion as early as 1945, three years before the first volume was published. While the mainstream New Naturalist volumes, at least in the early years, were intended to deal with broad subjects such as wild flowers, insects or National Parks, the new books, to be called 'monographs', would focus on specialist subjects such as ants, British reptiles or even single species such as the Badger or the Fulmar. They would, of course, share the same high standards of the main series and benefit from the library of colour images assembled by Collins and their partners, Adprint.

In practice, all but one of the first six published monographs was about species

of birds. The exception was *The Badger*. A schoolmaster in the Cotswolds, Ernest Neal, had, alone or with a team of enthusiastic young biology students, turned himself into, in his editors' words, 'a patient watchman' of badgers, as well as 'a cunning photographer, an ingenious detective and a careful judge'. He had spent a prodigious amount of time observing wild badgers and their ways, and he embodied the kind of naturalist the editors were looking for: a good observer, scientifically inclined, enthusiastic, outdoorsy and literate. Like many succeeding New Naturalist monographs, his was essentially the story of one man's passion for a wild animal.

The monographs were envisaged as relatively short books of 50,000 words or so, and in a smaller format than the main series. In February 1947, Clifford and Rosemary Ellis were asked to design jackets for the series. The jacket would need to declare the book's affinity with the New Naturalist library while clearly distinguishing them. The decision to put the title inside a coloured oval and to include a logo based on the letters NMN seems to have been taken in-house, though the actual logo was designed by C&RE. The jackets would be produced and printed in the same way as the parent series, in three or four colours.

The *Badger* jacket shows two striped heads emerging from the darkness, with a single, broad, clawed foot in the foreground. The colours – black, grey and pink – are appropriate to an animal normally seen only in the twilight around dusk; the pink is used mainly in overlaps to obtain a warm grey-brown and for the highlights on the animal's claws. In pure form it makes an eye-catching colour for the title, while the head of the second badger, seen from the front, produces an effective image for the spine. Unfortunately, the artists had been told that the book would be about an inch wide when it was barely half that. Hence the second badger's eyes are barely visible when the book is on the shelf. The Board minutes record that 'everyone thought [the jacket] was excellent'.

The sales of *The Badger* made a promising start to the monographs. Published in the late autumn of 1948, it remained in print for nearly thirty years, was translated into German and Japanese, and ran through five Collins editions as well as a mass-market Pelican paperback.

2 The Redstart *John Buxton, 1950*

The Redstart was the record of an Oxford academic's close study of a bird over five years while he was a prisoner of war in Germany. No one would normally have chosen a redstart as the most commercially viable subject for a monograph, but, of course, the editors were not really choosing subjects: they were choosing authors. John Buxton was a distinguished English scholar and a leading amateur ornithologist.

For the jacket C&RE made a number of pencil sketches based on photographs

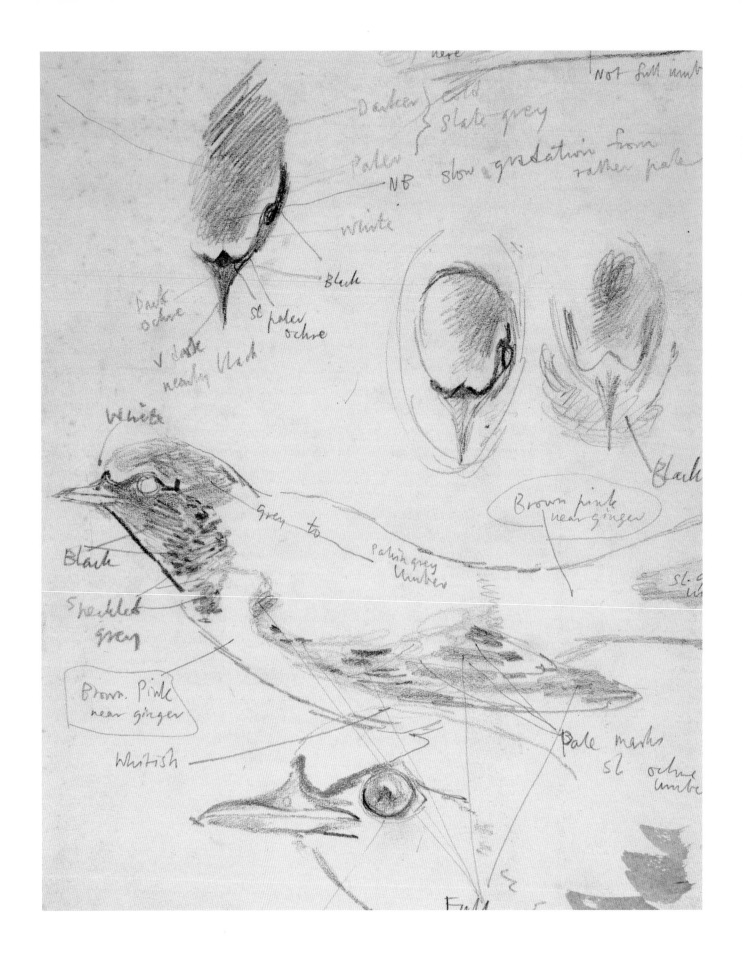

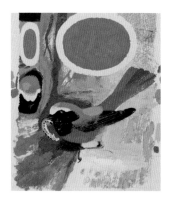

sent to them by the author. They show the bird full length and in close-up, with detailed notes on the colours. A sketch of the bird's head was transferred to the spine of the book, where it peeps through a hole in the wood. The full-length bird was shown in a more dynamic posture, emphasising the brightly coloured tail (the 'start' in 'redstart' comes from 'steort', Old English for 'tail'). C&RE chose a saturated rusty-red for the tail and teased out a range of tones for the background, a tangle of branches and hollow timbers. The printers experienced trouble in getting it exactly right, but the result was pleasing enough. The cock bird has returned to the nest with food; it might have been appropriate to show its mate waiting expectantly in its nest-hole, but this bird is in fact another cock redstart, perhaps the same one about to leave the nest. Completed in February 1948, the jacket not only places the redstart in its natural woodland setting but portrays an aspect of its behaviour.

John Buxton liked it, especially the spine: 'The head of the cock on the spine, popping out of its hole, is exactly right and most delightful!'

Stephen Moss, author, broadcaster and producer of BBC Television's *Springwatch* – as well as 'an inveterate NN collector' – writes:

'My favourite jacket? For me, it has to be one of the monographs, but which one? That pair of Hawfinches staring at each other like gargoyles? The citrus tones of *The Yellow Wagtail*, with a herd of cows grazing behind a giant bird? Or the equally vivid yellows of *The Wren*, whose subject virtually hops off the page? In the end, it has to be *The Redstart*, John Buxton's remarkable account of how he found freedom within a German POW camp by watching these birds. It was one of the first New Naturalists I bought. The image is so vibrant it is almost too big for the book, and the tail has to carry round to the flyleaf. The bright colours and the glint in the bird's eye bring the image to life. Looking at it afresh, the jacket conjures up memories of my all-too-infrequent sightings of this little gem of a bird. Simply magical.'

276

3 The Wren *Edward A. Armstrong, 1955*

Though given the number '3' in the series, *The Wren* was in fact the eleventh monograph in order of publication. The author had written a very long book about this smallest of birds. 'Who would read monographs of this length', wondered the non-ornithologist, Dudley Stamp, when he saw the size of the manuscript. William Collins was of similar mind, and demanded cuts. Even so, the setting costs exceeded the likely profits on the entire edition of 3,000. The ensuing controversy delayed the book's publication for several years.

For this unloved book C&RE designed one of their loveliest jackets, a study in browns and yellows of a wren's nest inside the wooden diamond of a trellis fence. The latter detail may have been inspired by the author's lyrical description of the moment when, as wartime bombers roared off into the winter night, 'a small bird [alighted] on the trellis outside and then [flew] up into the ivy on the wall'. The parent bird holds a tiny scrap in its beak which seems hardly enough to feed the four nestlings, all eyes and yellow gape as they beg for food from the spine of the book. The jacket, which was printed by Odhams of Watford, needed some adjustment, especially in the liveliness of the yellow, but the result pleased everybody.

Like *The Fulmar*, *The Wren* was published in standard New Naturalist size. More than most titles, it is hard to find this jacket in fresh condition since the pale colours become grubby with age, and it is prone to chipping and foxing. The condition of the average *Wren* jacket suggests that, *vade* Dudley Stamp's comment, those 3,000 or so people who bought *The Wren* did indeed read it.

4 The Yellow Wagtail *Stuart Smith, 1950*

Though it comes after *The Redstart* and *The Wren*, *The Yellow Wagtail* was in fact the first bird monograph to be completed and published. C&RE designed the jacket in spring 1948, possibly from photographs sent by the author (though the liveliest pictures in this book are the colour paintings by Edward Bradbury). The jacket shows a cock bird in summer plumage foraging in a field with cows grazing in the background. A second bird with a darker eye patch, perhaps its mate, makes an appearance on the spine. The background in tones of brown and green were calculated to make the bright yellow bird stand out all the more effectively.

James Fisher suggested a few improvements. The legs should be more prominent, and 'the whole of the claw should be flat on the ground', odd as it looked. 'The claw,' he explained, 'is lifted off in one movement, not as in walking, and the back leg is a little higher' (JF to CE, 29.9.48).

Unfortunately the printing let the design down. The intended tones were muddied and gave the impression of a bird wandering the field after sundown,

ABOVE RIGHT Full size pencil study of Yellow Wagtail on layout paper.

ABOVE Colour sketch (incomplete), full size, gouache and watercolour on layout paper with notes.

BOTTOM The full design of *The Yellow Wagtail*, including modification of legs and feet, full size, gouache and watercolour on watercolour paper, with printing instructions in pencil.

or under the blackest of storm clouds. This made the yellow, sun-like, oval look bizarre.

Two sets of proofs were made in February 1949, both unsatisfactory. 'It is, if you will forgive my saying so, partly your fault,' scolded Ruth Atkinson, 'because you used two browns, and I have tried to keep to four printings, and not five. I think we must stick to four for these Monographs, of which we do not print very large quantities … we will use the extra colour if it is absolutely necessary' (RA to CE, 2.2.49).

It seems that this jacket was printed to demand; my copy has 90p printed on the flyleaf, indicating it was printed after decimal currency was introduced in 1971.

5 The Greenshank *Desmond Nethersole-Thompson, 1951*

'Burn the jacket,' advised the naturalist Anthony Buxton. Reviewing the book for *The Spectator* in December 1951, he liked the book but hated C&RE's design: 'It is a brutal shame,' he railed, 'on the author (and on a greenshank) to have clothed this book in a vulgar jacket produced apparently by a pair of schoolchildren who have never seen the bird and never learned to draw.' Raleigh Trevelyan responded with a pledge to take 'great care in future that no New Naturalist books go to Anthony Buxton' (RT to CE, 14.1.52).

The *Greenshank* jacket fell foul not of any inability to draw but to cost constraints

278

and inexperience. Inspired by some posters by Charles Tunnicliffe for the RSPB that had been printed in only two colours, Trevelyan had asked the artists 'to have a shot at doing this design in two colours, to be reproduced in line'. If successful, the new, cheaper method might 'start a new style for the series and for you to abandon your policy of natural colours' (RT to CE, 21.2.51).

One of these colours would have to be green so the other would have to be black, or at least a contrasting dark colour. Such penny-pinching made it difficult to fit in with the author's suggestion of a greenshank displaying on a dead stump against a background of hills and pinewoods (with two more in flight in the background). The artists did, however, take note of his further suggestion of a bird standing in water emphasising 'the longish bill and green legs'.

This became the 'green shank' on the spine, a long green leg with the oval doing duty as the bird's body. C&RE did their best to enliven the design with tints and cross-hatching; 'the blockmaker must not attempt retouching,' warned Clifford, 'Our scribble in the lower part of the green block should be allowed to produce its own texture in the block' (CE, 24.3.51). The artists had departed from their usual policy, as requested, they produced colour separations to make life easier for the printer. The results were disappointing. Perhaps the poor reproduction was just as well for it stopped Trevelyan's dream of cheap two-colour jackets in its tracks.

Anyone who adopted Anthony Buxton's suggestion and burned the jacket was saying goodbye to around £150 in today's prices.

Des Thompson, son of the author and himself a distinguished ornithologist, writes:

'I don't remember my father commenting on the jacket, which is surprising since he tended to hold strong views on most matters – including the feel of his books. My mother thinks the jacket is fine, but says my father would have had to make do with it anyway, because Billy Collins tended to get his way on such matters.

'For my part, I dislike almost every aspect of it except one: the emphasis on the streaks on the bird's breast and neck feathers, and the exaggerated white fringes of the scapulas – but even here the detail is wrong, and the use of lime-green on the coverts and bill is hopeless (it implies they are the same colour as the olive-green legs, which they are not). The eye is too big, the flecks under the eye do not exist, the tertials and primaries are absent, the undertail-coverts are too prominent, and the leg is far too thick.

'When it comes to the backdrop, the greenshank is set against cross-hatched water, and the land behind has closely packed, vertical lines running into darkness, and descending from green, black and streaky-white beams, presumably depicting the elements of water, land and sky. There are no hints of pine trees, of rocks, or of the spacious landscapes occupied by this most graceful, excitable and agile of birds.

'No, sorry, in my view this is a disappointing jacket. I should say, though, that my brother Pat does like it, commenting that "the key thing you notice is the green legs – a deliberate corruption of the bird's legs and a play on the colour and name. It is actually very effective – it screams 'green' at you!"'

6 The Fulmar *James Fisher, 1952*

In February 1947, James Fisher wrote to Clifford to tell him of a book he was in the middle of writing. This was *The Fulmar*, the fruits of Fisher's obsession with 'the ghost-grey bird and green islands in grey seas'. The book was, according to his obituary, 'one of his proudest achievements – an extraordinary accumulation of information' – all 500-odd pages of it (and that was without the 2,378 supporting references!).

For the first version of the jacket, drawn in the standard monograph format, Fisher thought the artists had captured the bird well but asked for some changes:

the wings should not overlap or cross; the beak should be a little longer and more
hooked; the spot by the bird's eye should be more pronounced; and the egg
between its feet should be brought further forward. A little yellow webbing on the
feet might be a good idea, and, suggested Fisher, they might consider including a
few primroses dotted around the ledge as they are on St Kilda.

Their design had to be adjusted in any case for the new, larger format necessary
for this very long book. It incorporated most of Fisher's alterations except for the
primroses. 'We tried primroses but they seemed to break things up too much,' said
Clifford. The jacket's greys, blues and greens are soothing to the eye, though the
bird on the spine is more manic. c&re's fulmar is nesting at St Kilda, the ancestral
home of British fulmars. In the background are three islets in a row, intended to
represent the islets of Boreray, Stac Lee and Stac an Armin. Sixty years after

publication, most *Fulmar* jackets have toned spines but that now grubby bird was once as white as snow.

James Fisher was delighted with it: 'I would like to thank you personally for the cover,' he wrote. 'You can imagine what it means to me to have a cover of which, as a naturalist, I can approve. You have got the spirit of the bird absolutely, and it was a delightful touch to put in the shadowy figure of Boreray in the background – a touch that will be happily understood by the few who know it. It is a wonderful cover, and I wanted to tell you I thought so' (JF to CE, 30.9.1952).

The artwork for *The Fulmar* jacket was reputedly given away as a prize for the annual Bird Race in 1992.

7 **Fleas, Flukes and Cuckoos** *Miriam Rothschild and Theresa Clay, 1952*

William Collins was at a loss knowing what to do with this brilliant, oddball book. Under the working title of *Parasites of Birds*, the book was provisionally listed as a title in the mainstream series (it would have been New Naturalist No. 22). Later Billy Collins got cold feet about publishing a book on such a specialist subject, especially as the cost of production would be high in relation to likely sales. To begin with, C&RE were asked to design a jacket in the usual way; 'we would like a cuckoo on the front,' said Trevelyan, 'as we feel anything else might be a little macabre!' (RT to CE, 22.5.51). As with *The Greenshank*, they were asked to do the job in two colours, but this time without using colour separations. C&RE thereupon made a few preliminary pencil sketches for a cuckoo jacket.

Unfortunately, the book was in production at a time when the Ellises were busy with a multitude of other New Naturalist jackets. Because some of these were urgent, they were told not to bother, after all, with the jacket. We will 'think up an ordinary line jacket for this book', said Trevelyan (RT to CE, 3.7.51).

Poor *Fleas, Flukes*! Miriam Rothschild had independently commissioned another artist to design a jacket for it but was denied 'the pretty jacket I hankered after' (Marren, 2005). The book was published as a one-off 'special volume' in a cheap plain wrapper. Collins was completely wrong about the book's appeal. It sold out in two weeks.

8 **Ants** *Derek Wragge Morley, 1953*

Ants was the first monograph to be written; a version of it was ready in 1945. Unfortunately Wragge Morley's text was not peer-read by a fellow ant expert and the book, which was not published until 1953, received several poor reviews pointing out errors in the text. Legend has it that this book was thereupon withdrawn from sale. There is nothing about that in the record, and the truth seems to be that the

book sold out quite quickly and, like many of the monographs, was not reprinted.

Ants was another jacket that ran into trouble through various would-be cost-saving expedients. Raleigh Trevelyan had 'played around a little' with the artwork, and the only way he was able to move and reduce the size of the title ovals was to add grey paint to the top and bottom (RT to CE, 17.12.51). Then, unasked, the blockmakers at Odhams further touched up the original design. The jacket was printed by the 'line method' which filtered out the colours and resulted in harsh colour gradations with 'everything very sharp and black' (RT, *ibid.*).

Despite all this, the jacket was thought 'extremely attractive'. C&RE's ant is a red-brown wood-ant in its forest of grass blades, rearing up threateningly with open jaws. The sunny yellow of the title spot is echoed by lichen on the stone and the sunlight streaming through the grass.

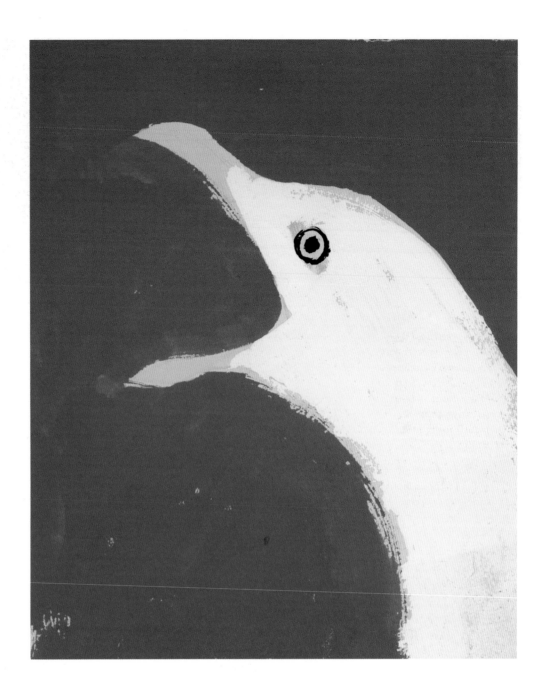

9 The Herring Gull's World *Niko Tinbergen, 1953*

Niko Tinbergen is the only Nobel Prize-winner among New Naturalist authors; his book, originally titled *A Herring Gull's World*, is perhaps the most influential, though not the most commercially successful, title in the series. It is a classic study in animal behaviour revealing a kind of avian psychology and the ways in which the gulls communicate with one another, with their mates and with their chicks. Despite its specialised nature, the book was true to the precepts of the series, being based on observation and simple experiments, and written in non-technical language.

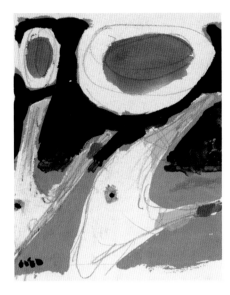

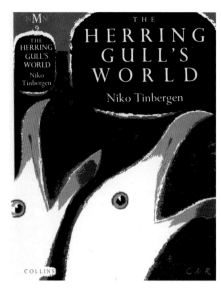

ABOVE Colour sketch for the jacket of *The Herring Gull's World* (left) in pencil and gouache paint on cartridge paper (¼ jacket size); full size design in pencil, black wax crayon and white paint (middle); the printed jacket (far right).

OPPOSITE Colour sketch of calling gull, gouache on buff sugar paper (18.5 × 15.3 cm).

The editors (Sir Julian Huxley was an eminent animal behaviourist) realised they had a winner on their hands, at least in academic terms. In 1953, however, this represented a new kind of book, and 'the sales people' wondered whether it was right for the series. Sensing that it was written primarily for university and college courses, they argued for publication outside the series, and in a plain wrapper. But, at Huxley's insistence, Billy Collins was persuaded to include it among the monographs, and an Ellis jacket was commissioned for it.

This subject interested Clifford, and the jacket he and Rosemary designed deliberately avoids showing us a straightforward bird portrait. Instead we are brought eye-to-eye with a 'vocalising' gull. There is no contact between bird and viewer: this is a wild bird with strange, alien motivations and habits, and to find out just how strange, says the jacket, you will need to open the book. Colour sketches survive, showing how the artists experimented with gulls' heads before arriving at a simple yet effective way of conveying the contents of the book. Their only mistake, if mistake it was, was to overestimate its width, so that most of the eye of the second gull misses the spine.

The jacket was a success. 'Everyone is v. thrilled by [it],' said Trevelyan, 'and we think it is a real winner. I consider the production has turned out well' (RT to CE, 4.9.53).

10 Mumps, Measles and Mosaics *Kenneth M. Smith and Roy Markham, 1954*

A book about the invisible viruses that cause disease in animals and plants was never going to be a winner. Like *Fleas, Flukes and Cuckoos,* the title was a clear attempt to make the book sound intriguing. The 'sales people' had even more doubts about this book than with *Fleas, Flukes,* and it was only included in the series at the Board's insistence. Collins compromised by calling it a 'special volume' and

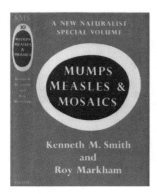

denying it an illustrated jacket (and allowing it only one measly colour plate). The design of the *Mumps, Measles* jacket is the same as *Fleas, Flukes*, but, since this is a shorter book, it is in smaller 'monograph' format.

Unlike *Fleas, Flukes*, it sold slowly, perhaps mainly to libraries and agricultural colleges. The book was out of stock by the end of the 1950s and was not reprinted.

11 **The Heron** *Frank A. Lowe, 1954*

Most people like this lively jacket with its riot of eyeballs and beaks. The cue for the design was a remark by Raleigh Trevelyan that 'an ordinary heron standing on one leg in the middle of a river is rather too trite. Can you let us have a design of a heronry?' he asked, adding: 'This might be rather unusual and striking … I don't suppose it would be possible for you to do it in two colours this time?' (RT to CE, 1.4.53).

Design sketches for *The Heron* jacket. Gouache and pencil on thin card (24.5 × 30.5 cm).

The last time c&re had designed a two-colour jacket, for *The Greenshank*, the result had been disappointing. Fortunately, the heron is essentially a two-tone bird in shades of grey, black and white. The bird's characteristic neck pattern might look nice on the spine suggested the author, Frank Lowe.

The artists' solution was to show the head of the parent bird on a horizontal plane with the begging chicks pointing upwards. It made a pleasing pattern and they made the most of the chick's fuzzy heads and fishy white eyes. There was just room to show the heron's characteristic hackle feathers on the bottom right. The jacket was printed by Odhams, and although it uses only dark colours, grey and black, the result is far from gloomy.

12 Squirrels *Monica Shorten, 1954*

In general birds (and reptiles) lend themselves better to jacket designs than mammals. The modelling of a mammal's head (unless shown in silhouette) is difficult to achieve with the flat planes of lithography, and fur is harder to suggest than scales or feathers.

The *Squirrels* jacket bears this out. c&re had been given the choice of grey or red squirrels (with a request from the author that the former be 'not too ugly'). They chose the red, but the anatomy is all wrong: the eyes are too far forward and too close together, and the skull is too narrow. And the tail looks as though it is on fire. This was a pity since the background to the image is rich and varied, with the

287

branches and trunk nicely marbled with tints of red, ochre and black.

The printer had used a heavy tone of brown for the squirrel, giving an unwanted sense of weight. 'Odham's effort seems a bit of a shock,' said Raleigh Trevelyan (RT to CE, 9.6.54). The blockmaker rejoined that the squirrel design was one of the most complicated he had ever had, and the colours were difficult to match exactly.

Despite these troubles, the *Squirrels* jacket, along with *Sea-Birds*, was exhibited by the National Book League as one of the best of that year's book jacket designs.

13 The Rabbit *Harry V. Thompson and Alastair N. Worden, 1956*

For this austere monograph, C&RE drew a very uncuddly rabbit. To further rub in the message that the New Naturalist rabbit was not at all like Beatrix Potter's, a skull sits on the spine. The rabbit of 1956 was both a serious agricultural pest (the book's working title had been *The Rabbit and the Rabbit Problem*) and a victim – of myxomatosis. Hideously deformed, dead or dying rabbits were being found everywhere. Collins rushed out the book to cash in on the myxomatosis scare.

The preliminary sketches show that the artists intended from the start to portray a frontal view of the animal's head. They are drawn from life with careful attention given to the lashes, whiskers and nostrils. The final design is more stylised, with extraneous detail stripped away, leaving dark eyes staring blankly at the reader, and a pair of outsize ears supporting the oval of the title.

'Congratulations on *The Rabbit*, which is enthusiastically accepted,' wrote Raleigh Trevelyan (RT to CE, 2.9.55). The National Book League chose this jacket, along with

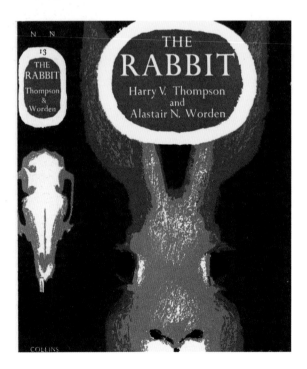

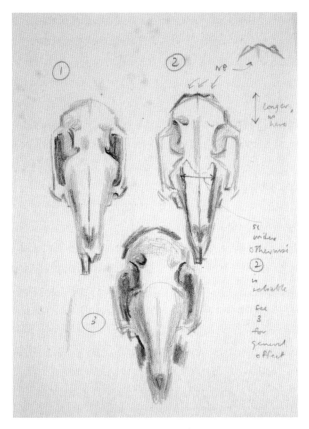

Pencil and colour studies for *The Rabbit* jacket: three skulls with pencil notes (21 × 14 cm).

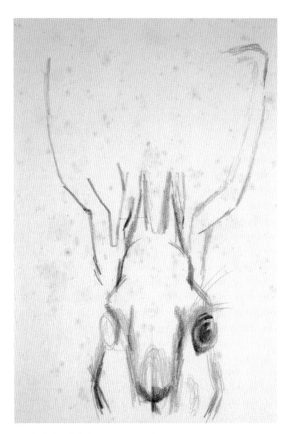

Rabbit's head, full size as on jacket.

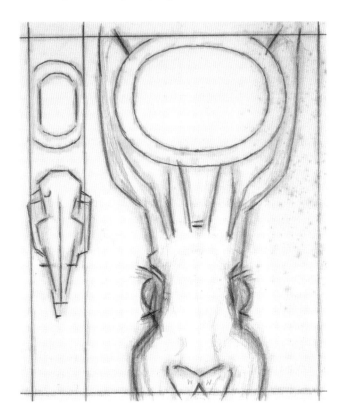

Pencil design for the jacket on typing paper, full size.

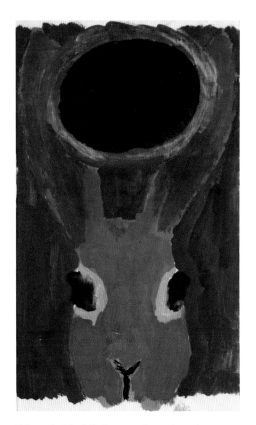

Colour sketch, full size, gouache on layout paper.

Mountain Flowers, for their exhibition at the Victoria and Albert Museum in 1956. 'Studies and colour sketches for *The Rabbit* and *The Folklore of Birds*' were also exhibited in 1990 in 'The Decorative Beast' by the Crafts Council, London.

14 Birds of the London Area Since 1900 *R. C. Homes and the London Natural History Society, 1957*

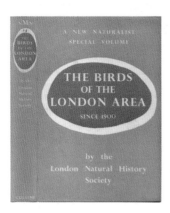

This misfit of a book is the odd-man-out of the monographs and a strange subject for a New Naturalist monograph. The idea was to include it as a 'special volume' as a kind of pendant to *London's Natural History*. William Collins was reluctantly persuaded to publish it once the London Natural History Society undertook to purchase some for sale to its members. As the author-editor Richard Homes justifiably exclaimed, the offered terms 'seem incredibly hard bargaining for a firm of your standing', but, even so, Collins made only £85 profit from it (some monographs, notably *The Wren*, made a loss).

The book was eventually re-published on a more satisfactory basis by Rupert Hart-Davis in 1964. But, of course, the book the collectors want is not this one but its ill-fated New Naturalist predecessor in its plain green wrapper.

15 The Hawfinch *Guy Mountfort, 1957*

Yet another uncommercial book about a little-known bird: no wonder Billy Collins was losing faith in the monographs. For *The Hawfinch*, it seems that someone (not he) was determined to cut their losses by printing the book on the cheap. The paper quality was poorer than usual so that the print showed through at the chapter ends, and Keith Shackleton's beautiful scraperboard drawings reproduced poorly. To add insult to injury, the pages were accidentally undercut leaving the page trim (and hence the binding) slightly smaller than the standard monograph size.

The economy extended to the jacket. Few exactly match the size of the book, and most are slightly shorter as though the jacket had shrunk. Towards the end of the print-run it seems the supply ran out, and, reluctant to print more, Collins wrapped the remaining stock in green 'sugar paper' (the internal file calls them 'plain cellophane wrappers'). The design itself was generally admired: 'we are delighted with *The Hawfinch*,' wrote Trevelyan (RT to CE, 6.6.56). Unfortunately, the rich reddish-brown ink is light-sensitive and most copies of *The Hawfinch* now show some fading on the spine.

C&RE's design focuses on the bird's most notable feature, its massive bill, capable of cracking cherry stones. They used a rich chestnut for the bird's head which almost glows against a dark grey background. Two hawfinches glower at one another, their beaks almost touching. What are they doing? Read on.

Andrew Branson, naturalist and publisher of *British Wildlife*, writes:

'These two hawfinches, caught in a curious "kissing" of bills, have nestled on my bookshelves since the mid-1960s. Like all great jacket artwork, the image is immediately arresting, but also puzzling. Are the birds sparring males or a male courting his partner? The grotesque bills are the focus of the design, their dense outlines arching across the jacket. The Ellises undoubtedly picked up on a memorable passage in the monograph where Guy Mountfort describes the measuring of the immense crushing force of the bird's bill at the National Physical Laboratory (with the help of fresh olive stones flown in specially from Palestine). In a later chapter the author observes how a pair of courting hawfinches touched bills for a fraction of a second at which the female sprang away "as though electrified". Perhaps the jacket captures this rarely witnessed intimate moment in the lives of these elusive birds.'

16 The Salmon *J. W. Jones, 1959*

The Salmon was the first of two monographs about fish, the other being *The Trout*. Eric Hosking had suggested the title, pointing out that it had a large potential market among fly-fishermen (William Collins, himself a keen country sportsman, also published fishing books). Despite its dry text and dim illustrations, the book did well enough to be reprinted several times (and with a small US edition). Consequently *The Salmon* and *The Trout* are among the most frequently found New Naturalist monographs on the book market today.

A jacket showing an entire salmon might have looked insipid. C&RE decided instead to show just the head and shoulders of an old male fish. Limited to three colours – blue, green and black – they could not show the salmon in its true pink breeding colours nor give much sense of fast-flowing water. What they could do was to suggest the bulk of a large fish with its fins and scales, and above all the

Two studies of salmon heads, pencil on cartridge paper (35 × 26 cm).

OPPOSITE Artwork for *The Salmon* jacket with printing instructions.

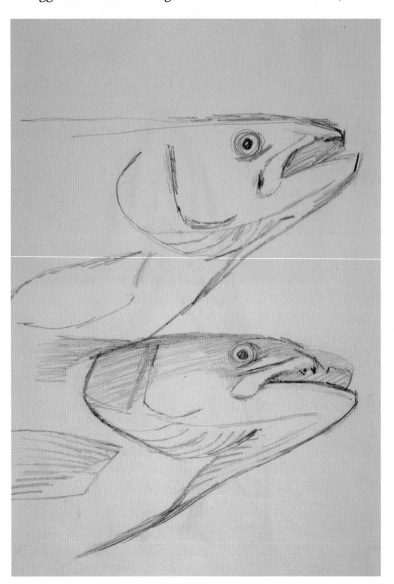

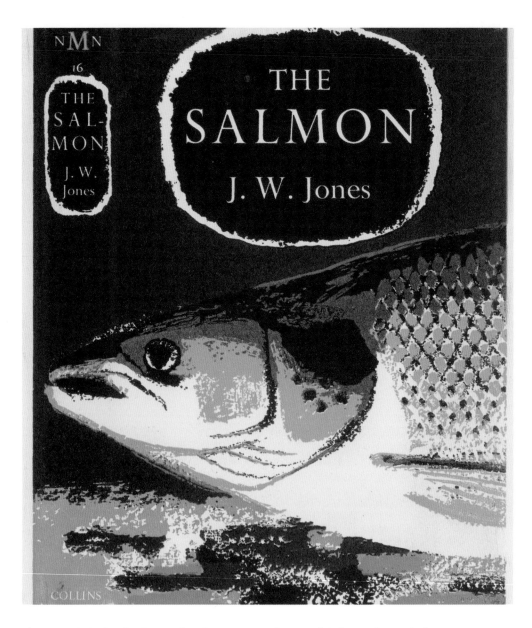

characteristic hooked mouth of a mature salmon which was intended to curve over onto the spine. Unfortunately, this was another thin book, and on some copies the fish's jaws pass right over the spine to end up on the back. The work needed some alterations to the salmon's eye and head shape, and to cover up some teeth. Trevelyan was 'pleased to accept' the revised version in April 1955 – four years before the book was eventually published.

17 Lords & Ladies *Cecil T. Prime, 1960*

Lords & Ladies is the only botanical monograph (unless you count the plant mosaics in *Mumps, Measles*). Devoted to a single common species, our wild arum lily, the book has become a minor classic, one of the few rounded scientific

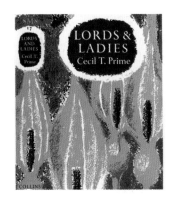

portraits of any plant. Such was its reputation that the book was later reprinted by BSBI Publications in association with the author's widow. Unfortunately, disappointing sales precluded more plant monographs, though the book's schoolmaster author, Cecil T. Prime, was keen to write at least two more, on primroses and thistles. In terms of print-run, *Lords & Ladies* is the rarest of all the monographs with sales of only about 2,400 over ten years.

The jacket, which was ready by January 1960, was liked by Billy Collins but, for some reason, was 'not admired' by the Board. John Gilmour received a mild rebuke for not having checked the artist's sketch from a botanical viewpoint: 'It was agreed that all wrapper roughs must be approved by the editor concerned'. The sketch survives, a carefully painted group of lords-and-ladies against a dark background with their glorious purple spadices contrasting well with their pale-green hoods. For the finished jacket the same design is rendered more freely with smudged outlines in two shades of green plus purple (with black for the oval). It is as nice a design as one could wish for and one wonders what the editors found to 'not admire' about it.

ABOVE The printed jacket of *Lords & Ladies.*

RIGHT Artwork with pencilled printing instructions.

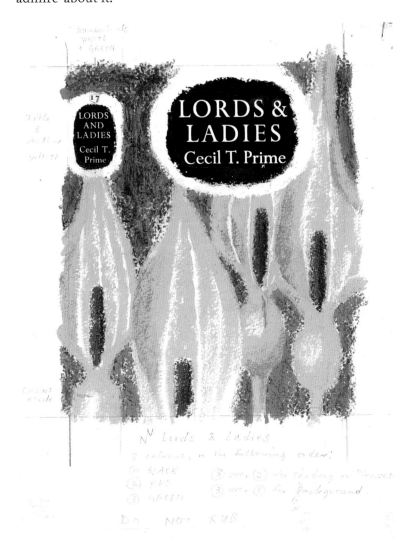

Numerals
etc
RED +
GREEN

Title
&
Author
WHITE

COLLINS
White

N Lords & Ladies

3 colours printed in the following
order:

BLACK   Green over Red makes
RED   brownish green
GREEN   Green over Black
               for background.

DO NOT RUB

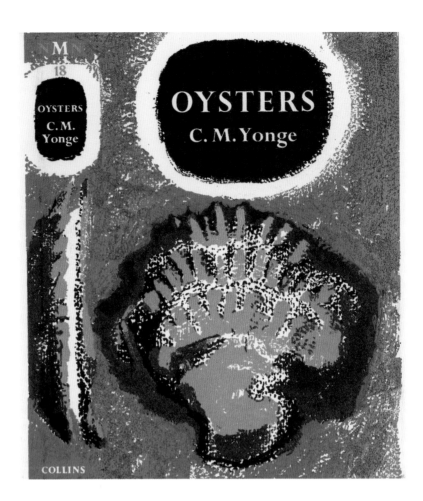

18 Oysters *C. M. Yonge, 1960*

Oysters are a difficult title for a book jacket. Unlike, say, scallops or cockles, their shells have no well-defined pattern or form other than being rough and vaguely fan-shaped. Nor do oysters exhibit the kind of behaviour that lends itself to a drawing, still less a three-colour jacket. The only way to be sure that a shell is an oyster is to show someone swallowing one.

The artists stuck to their brief of showing the object of the book close-up and without distracting detail. They simply showed a shell seen from above, and, on the spine, from the side. Whether anyone would recognise the Ellises' oyster without the title in large white letters above it may be doubted (to me it looks more like a scallop shell). But the colours – olive-green, black and an uncharacteristic bright blue, presumably representing the ocean – are bold and bright, and the smudgy image is certainly eye-catching.

'Odhams had great difficulty with it,' noted the current editor, Jean Whitcombe, 'so I hope you will be pleased with it' (JW to CE, 25.4.60). But the editors all liked it, and 'so did Prof. Yonge, the author' (JW to CE, 2.8.60).

19 The House Sparrow *J. D. Summers-Smith, 1963*

Although it was the tenth bird monograph to appear, *The House Sparrow* is the one that most lives up to the editors' aim of publishing studies of significant species. In 1963 the sparrow was our most familiar wild bird, especially in towns and cities. Yet, since birders tend to prefer more exotic species in wilder places (as some of the monographs bear out), it had been neglected. Dennis Summers-Smith's now classic book was the first one ever published about the House Sparrow. Because of its length, a 'standard biography' format (i.e. the size of *The World of the Honeybee*) was briefly considered for the book before opting for the standard monograph format.

C&RE began by sketching House Sparrows from life. They worked up some of these into possible designs, starting with the whole bird, before finally choosing one that showed only the head. This is a sparrow pared down to essentials, in its handsome chestnut, grey and black colours the powerful bill, and open as if in mid-chirrup. The spine shows a second sparrow bathing with fluffed up feathers and a happy look on its face. The design artwork was ready in March 1962, and was well received. Compared with the fuss over some of those printed in the early 1950s one is struck by the smoothness in which these later jackets went through.

20 The Wood Pigeon *R. K. Murton, 1965*

Ron Murton used to do a wonderful impersonation of the Wood Pigeon as it pecked and bobbed its way through the clover field. Some of his humour and liveliness survives in *The Wood Pigeon*, but this is a serious book, and, like *The Rabbit*, one written by a professional ecologist from an agricultural viewpoint. The science may be impeccable but the distance between the observer and the observed has grown.

The Wood Pigeon is classed as an injurious bird mainly because it likes the same things that we do – such as cabbages, sprouts, turnips and kale. With a nice touch of wit, C&RE chose to show the pigeon along with its recent meal, a stripped-down cabbage leaf. The bird's coloration allowed them to use a beautiful warm grey-blue, with a bright yellow used in pure form solely for the bird's eye (the green of the cabbage leaf is yellow on top of blue-grey). It is a quiet design, and the pigeon's expression is innocence itself.

No correspondence survives for this jacket; presumably, then, production was problem-free.

21 The Trout *W. E. Frost and M. E. Brown, 1967*

The Trout took a long time to write: commissioned in 1946, it was not published until 1967. The title was to have been *The Brown Trout*, but, it seems, the 'Brown' bit was dropped after Margaret Brown joined her colleague, Winifred Frost, as co-author. Perhaps two 'Browns' might have been confusing.

The Trout was a better book than *The Salmon*: more readable, more broad-ranging and better illustrated. And c&re gave it a better jacket. Letting in a lot of white on their favourite turquoise gave an impressionistic sense of rippling water. Three trout move through the current but none is shown full length. They are not individuals but members of a shoal, and they are facing upstream to let the water flow through their gills. The fish are painted very freely in grey with brown overlaps and flecks of black from a dry brush; close-up their shapes almost dissolve. At the authors' request, the artists straightened the fish's tail. The revised design was ready by January 1964. c&re hoped that the delicate colours of this jacket would print well. Unfortunately the inks were too opaque to capture the full sense of the trout's watery world. However, everybody liked it.

Colour sketches for *The Trout* jacket, gouache on typing paper (6.5 × 17 cm).

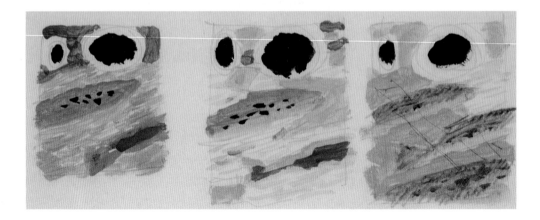

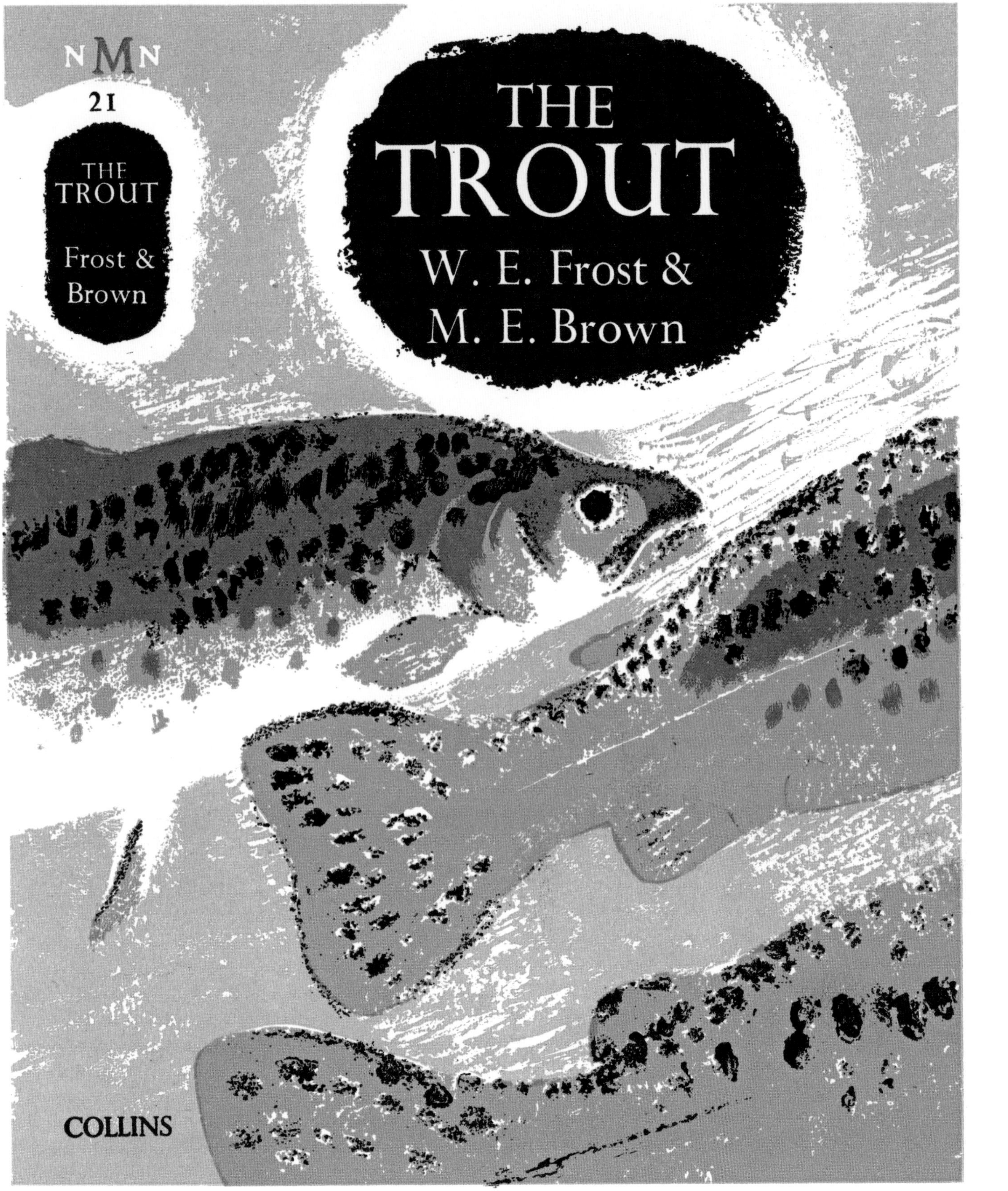
NMN
21
THE
TROUT
Frost &
Brown
THE
TROUT
W. E. Frost &
M. E. Brown
COLLINS

OPPOSITE Colour separations for *The Mole* jacket for each of the four colours.

22 The Mole *Kenneth Mellanby, 1971*

The last of the monographs was about author Kenneth Mellanby's favourite animal, the mole (he also wrote a children's book, *Talpa the Mole*). By 1971 the monographs had more or less run their course; most were out of print or about to become so. Only *The Badger*, *The Herring Gull's World* and the two fish books had been commercial successes, while for some of the others the publishers had actually made a loss. Mellanby was by now a New Naturalist editor, and the mole was a subject which had been on the stocks since the 1940s. The book became another of the successful monographs, thanks to a big Reader's Union edition (printed in grey boards without the Collins imprint), which remained in print until 1980. Fine copies of the book are relatively easy to find.

For this swan-song monograph, C&RE created one of their most disturbing jackets, a sharp-toothed Dracula of a Mole heaving itself from the earth at night.

302

NN Monograph
The MOLE
(2) Brown

NN Monograph
The MOLE
(4) Pink

NMN on spine = white
~~the N white on this block~~
~~the 2 N's overprinted~~

Collins = white

NN Monograph
The MOLE
(1) Dark blue

NN Monograph
The MOLE

Colours with pencil notes attached by the artists to colour separations to guide the printer.

The design is cleverly done, using overlaps of colours to produce a rich, velvety tone for the animal's fur. It was daring of them to create quite such an unlovely mole. The cue for the jacket may have come from the new editor, Michael Walter (with whom Clifford always seems to have got on well). 'You'll know the mole's interesting system of burrows and castles or underground nesting chambers,' he wrote teasingly to Clifford, 'but since it is pitch darkness down there, it will be of little interest to you' (MW to CE, 15.1.71). The artists' solution was to show the animal as it leaves its burrow, as if caught in a spotlight.

With *Man & Birds*, this was the first jacket to be printed from a set of four colour separations prepared by the artists with black brushwork on thick white paper. Production was problematic. The grey and pink colours were hard to match accurately since they required a lot of white, which increased their opacity. When he saw the first proof, Clifford commented that the pink and grey were too dark and the latter colour also insufficiently warm. This affected the design, notably the modelling of the head and feet, and the tone and colour of the soil which needed to be lighter and warmer than the animal's fur. Although the jacket was proofed a second time, not all of these problems were overcome.

After *The Mole*, titles that might once have been published as New Naturalist monographs, such as *British Seals*, and the commissioned but never-published *The Fox*, were listed as mainstream titles. For birds at least, the monographs now faced direct competition from the titles published by T. & A. D. Poyser. Yet there is nothing in the record to suggest a sudden cessation of the series. The monographs seem to have quietly faded away for want of decision and direction.

Notes

p 12 Paul Ayshford, Lord Methuen (1886–1974), R. A., F. S. A., M. A., Hon. LL. D., Hon. F. R. I. B. A., P P R W A, was a key figure in the Ellises' professional career and a prominent figure in art and conservation circles: Trustee of the Tate and National Galleries and Imperial War Museum, Monuments Officer in the Allied Forces, Monuments, Fine Arts and Archives Branch principally in Normandy, then in Belgium and Holland (August 1944–June 1945), member of the Royal Fine Art Commission (1952–59), he played an active role in the nascent National Trust and served on their Historic Buildings Committee. He was a frequent exhibitor, and a President of the Bath Society of Artists.

p 15 Corsham Court was altered and enlarged in the eighteenth century, most notably, in 1761, by Capability Brown, who not only landscaped the park but designed new interiors including the 72-feet-long east wing picture gallery to house the celebrated Sir Paul Methuen collection of old masters. In 1800, the house was again remodelled in a more picturesque Gothic style by Nash and Repton with a new north front and further Picture Gallery, yet by the 1840s, their north front required rebuilding and from 1845 to 1849 Thomas Bellamy made the final Jacobean-Renaissance-inspired alterations, including the great stair tower.

References

Bath Academy of Art. Prospectus, 1953–54.

Bernstein, David (ed.) (1992). Introduction. *The Shell Poster Book*. Hamish Hamilton, London.

Brown, David (ed.) (1989). Introduction. Exhibition catalogue. 'Corsham: A Celebration. The Bath Academy of Art, 1946–72'. Michael Parkin Gallery, London.

Cook, Brian (1987). *The Britain of Brian Cook: A Batsford Heritage*. Batsford, London.

Ellis, Clifford (1981). Taped interview with Lucy Havelock for Imperial War Museum. 'Artists in an Age of Conflict' series.

Ellis, Clifford and Rosemary (revised edition) (1945). *Modelling for Amateurs*. 'How to do It' series, No. 20. The Studio Ltd, London.

Gillmor, Robert (2006). *Cutting Away. The Linocuts of Robert Gillmor*. Langford Press, Peterborough.

Griffits, T. E. (1956). *The Rudiments of Lithography*. Faber & Faber, London.

Griffits, T. E. (1948). *The Technique of Colour Printing by Lithography*. Faber & Faber, London.

Hendy, Philip (1947). Introduction. *A Catalogue of Lithographs*. Lyons & Co, London.

Marren, Peter (2nd edition) (2005). *The New Naturalists*. Collins, London.

Rennie, Paul (2008). 'The New Publicity: Design Reform, Commercial Art and Design Education 1910–39'. In: *London Transport Posters. A Century of Art and Design*, Eds. David Bownes & Oliver Green, London Transport Museum.

Thompson, Colin (1986). Unpublished paper, subsequently published in: Appendices. *A Celebration of Bath Academy of Art at Corsham*. Ed Derek Pope, 1997.

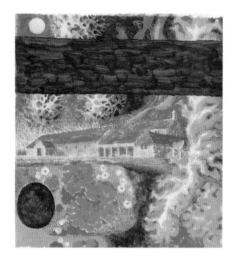

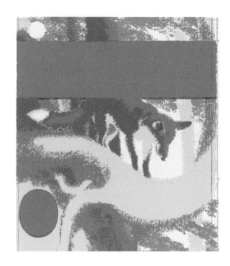

Unpublished Jackets

During the 1970s, C&RE designed jackets for several New Naturalist titles that were, for one reason or another, never published. At this stage the designs were all prepared from colour separations which were then combined photograph-ically by the printer to produce the completed jacket. To guide the printer, the artists usually produced a colour sketch of the design which, although it gave only a rough idea of its final form, reproduced the desired colours accurately. Jackets were never printed for these missing titles but fortunately the sketches were preserved and so can be reproduced here. Using today's computing technology, it would now be possible to combine the surviving colour separations to produce an even more accurate representation of what these jackets might have looked like.

LICHENS

C&RE designed two different versions of a New Naturalist on lichens (above left and centre), one a view of a building beyond a lichen-covered wall and overhanging branch and the other a close-up of lichens on a stone wall. The book was commissioned in 1972 when it was hoped that Dr Peter James, then at the Natural History Museum, would find time to write it. By the early 1980s, plans for the title had changed and it was projected as a symposium-like production with multiple authors edited into a seamless whole by Dr Mark Seaward. This book was published elsewhere, but the New Naturalist lichen book was eventually brought to a triumphant conclusion by Oliver Gilbert in 1999, and given a Robert Gillmor jacket.

THE FOX

The Fox was originally intended to be a New Naturalist monograph, but its eventual jacket design indicates that it was later promoted to the mainstream series. A string of distinguished authors had been asked to write it, and a full text was eventually completed in 1974 by H. G. Lloyd. It was at this stage that C&RE were asked to design a jacket and came up with this sketch of an alert-looking fox looking down from what appears to be a branch. Unfortunately the text was over-long, and, for this and other reasons, the book was withdrawn and published elsewhere (as *The Red Fox*, Batsford, 1980). Had it remained in the series, *The Fox* might have weighed in at about number 60, next to *British Birds of Prey*.

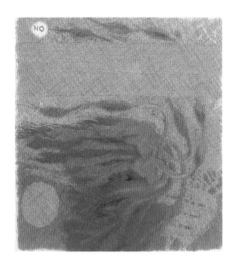

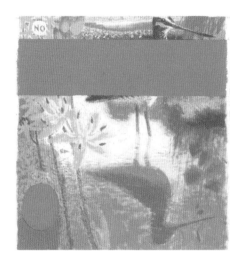

SEAWEEDS

This striking jacket sketch of kelp fronds swaying in the tide was probably drawn in the mid-1970s after Dr William Eifion Jones (1925–2004), a Welsh marine botanist, had been commissioned to write a New Naturalist on seaweeds. Unusually C&RE draw it in crayons instead of gouache paint. Unfortunately the book was never finished, and the title was temporarily dropped from the series in 1984.

WAYSIDES

This was to have been a volume about the wild plants and animals of tracks, roadside verges and railway lines. The commissioned author was the coincidentally named Dr Michael Way, then part of the distinguished Monks Wood scientific team that had already authored *Hedges, Pesticides and Pollution* and *Man & Birds*. C&RE designed this lovely jacket in the mid-1970s, probably at around the same time as *Bogs and Fens* and *Seaweeds*.

BOGS AND FENS

A New Naturalist about peat bogs was first suggested in the early 1960s by a then unknown university botany lecturer called David Bellamy (there is a file note to say that 'we must find out more about Bellamy'). The book, expanded to *Bogs and Fens*, and then *Wetlands*, was pencilled in as a desired title, and at one point it was hoped that David Goode, then assistant Chief Scientist in the Nature Conservancy Council, would find time to write it. This attractive jacket sketch by C&RE featuring Snipe and Bog Asphodel was probably drawn in the mid-1970s.

Index

Entries in *italics* indicate photographs and illustrations.